"Each subject in school is built upon words that bring forth meaning to students and our communities. At the center is vocabulary – language used to make communication possible. *Assessing Students with Poetry Writing Across Content Areas* promotes the power of language in poetic forms to formatively and summatively assess content knowledge within the classroom. Through mentor texts and models across a variety of poetic genres (acrostics, pantoums, free-verse, sevenlings, hy(na)kus, etc.), Donovan and her team demonstrate that poetry encourages young people to think, rationalize, and reason. Each chapter honors student voice, creativity, and agency while showcasing the ways poetry can be used to enhance discourse communities. The authors provide pathways for bridging interdisciplinary and content-focused possibilities through questions, inquiry, content-specific vocabulary, and critical thinking. I can't wait to bring these humanizing practices to the teacher institutes I lead, the courses I teach, and the youth programs I host."
- **Bryan Ripley Crandall**, *Director of the Connecticut Writing Project and Professor of English Education at Fairfield University*

"*Assessing Students with Poetry Writing Across Content Areas* not only provides a plethora of lessons and assessment guides (which can be modified) for all secondary content areas, but the authors, all veteran teachers from a variety of disciplines, share real experiences of transitioning to humanized assessment practices – yes, even in math! Acknowledging that teachers are, in fact, content area experts and the most significant determinant of learning in the classroom, the authors provide ways to bring the joy of learning into content assessment for both teachers and students. Additionally, this text offers a means to push back against the ever-growing GAI movement by engaging students through authentic reading, writing, and thinking processes that build needed skills and background knowledge all while retaining their voice. I highly encourage teachers and teacher educators to play with the assessment practices in this book. I know I will be using it in my pre-service teaching courses."
- **Michele McConnell**, *Ph.D., 17-year veteran high school teacher and Assistant Professor of English Studies at CSU Fresno.*

"There are so many critical elements to assessment and teaching in the content areas that the authors of *Assessing Students with Poetry Writing Across Content Areas: Humanizing Formative Assessment for Grades 6-12* include in their text. I greatly appreciate the re-calibration on how formative assessment should be viewed and can be utilized in secondary classrooms. Using poetry as a means of formative assessment and to promote engagement is powerful, for both striving and advanced readers. Using poetry and encouraging writing across the content areas promotes deep learning and culturally responsive teaching.

As an instructor at both the undergraduate and graduate levels of content area literacy courses, I value the different lenses through which each of the chapter authors discuss writing, content area learning, and formative assessment to provide a fit for classrooms 6-12 across a wealth of subjects. The sample poems and suggestions for what and how to write poetry are helpful, as is the wealth of poetry included throughout the text. This is a resource that teachers can take into their classroom tomorrow to start teaching authentically and critically, to prepare students for successful thinking and composition at any academic level."

- **Aileen Hower**, *Ed.D., Associate Professor of Literacy Content Area Literacy Instructor, Millersville University of Pennsylvania, Co-Author,* Centering ELLs in the Science of Reading *(Quick Reference Guide), ASCD*

"This book takes an asset-based and humanizing approach to assessment. The authors consider the aim of assessment to determine what students know and can do and also as a tool for teachers to determine the next instructional steps. In an age where data-informed decisions are highly valued, the approach in this book helps readers broaden their understanding of what counts as data and how students can demonstrate learning in creative and culturally sustaining ways. Specifically, the

authors showcase field-tested lessons using poetry for formative and summative assessment in their secondary content area classrooms. This book is a great resource for content teachers looking to support their students' critical and creative thinking through writing and looking for ways to enhance their use of assessment to inform instruction."
  - **Shea Kerkhoff**, *Associate Professor of Literacy and Secondary Education, University of Missouri-St. Louis*

Assessing Students with Poetry Writing Across Content Areas

Assessing Students with Poetry Writing Across Content Areas reimagines formative assessment by advocating for a dynamic, poetic approach that delves into students' meaning-making processes. It is a guide for teachers seeking innovative approaches to formative assessment, promoting a holistic, creative, reflective, and collaborative learning environment. It challenges the limitations of traditional worksheets and quizzes, urging educators to move beyond seeking restrictive answers and embrace students' texts as pathways to understanding.

The authors put forward poetry as a vigorous tool and writing poetry as an act to foster deep learning across content areas. Practical examples of acrostic poems, haiku, and pantoum demonstrate the adaptability of poetic forms to diverse subjects. Through adaptable lesson plans that can be used across history, math, world languages, ELA, and science, the book encourages intentional poetic writing-to-learn activities and explores how poetry might present itself as a short, creative assessment tool that helps teachers see what their students know and can do while also offering them the space to make new meaning in their original poetry.

This book is a key resource for in-service educators teaching grades 6-12.

Sarah J. Donovan has over 20 years of teaching experience in grades 6-20 and is an Associate Professor of Secondary Education English at Oklahoma State University. She teaches pre-service and in-service teacher courses and leads professional development across the country in humanizing English language arts pedagogy. Her research focuses on the lifespan of teachers.

Kim Johnson has taught for over three decades in public and private schools at all grades from preschool through secondary grades and currently serves as the District Literacy Specialist for Pike County School System in Zebulon, Georgia.

Anna J. Small Roseboro is a National Board Certified Teacher and National Writing Project Fellow with 40 years of experience, living and working in five states, teaching English Language Arts and Public Speaking to middle school, high school, and college students in public and private schools.

Barbara Edler is a Composition Instructor and Writer and taught high school English, Speech and Drama, and Talented and Gifted students for over 42 years.

Gayle Sands is currently a Professional Development School Liaison at McDaniel College. She previously served 27 years as a Middle School ELA teacher and Reading Specialist in Carroll County, MD.

Also Available from Routledge Eye On Education
(www.routledge.com/eyeoneducation)

Teaching Poetry in a Digital World: Inspiring Poetry Writing through Technology in Grades 6-12
Stefani Boutelier and Sarah J. Donovan

Teaching Reading and Literature with Classroom Talk: Dialogical Approaches and Practical Strategies in the Secondary ELA Classroom
Dawan Coombs

Teach This Poem, Volume I: The Natural World
Madeleine Fuchs Holzer and The Academy of American Poets

Student-Centered Literacy Assessment in the 6-12 Classroom: An Asset-Based Approach
Sean Ruday

Grammar Inquiries, Grades 6–12: An Inquiry- and Asset-Based Approach to Grammar Instruction
Sean Ruday

The Antiracist English Language Arts Classroom
Keisha Rembert

The Literacy Coaching Handbook: Working With Teachers to Increase Student Achievement, 2nd edition
Diana Sisson and Betsy Sisson

Assessing Students with Poetry Writing Across Content Areas

Humanizing Formative Assessment for Grades 6-12

Sarah J. Donovan, Kim Johnson,
Anna J. Small Roseboro, Barbara Edler, and
Gayle Sands

NEW YORK AND LONDON

Designed cover image: © Getty Images

First published 2026
by Routledge
605 Third Avenue, New York, NY 10158

and by Routledge
4 Park Square, Milton Park, Abingdon, Oxon, OX14 4RN

Routledge is an imprint of the Taylor & Francis Group, an informa business

© 2026 Sarah J. Donovan, Kim Johnson, Anna J. Small Roseboro, Barbara Edler, and Gayle Sands

The right of Sarah J. Donovan, Kim Johnson, Anna J. Small Roseboro, Barbara Edler, and Gayle Sands to be identified as authors of this work has been asserted in accordance with sections 77 and 78 of the Copyright, Designs and Patents Act 1988.

All rights reserved. No part of this book may be reprinted or reproduced or utilised in any form or by any electronic, mechanical, or other means, now known or hereafter invented, including photocopying and recording, or in any information storage or retrieval system, without permission in writing from the publishers.

Trademark notice: Product or corporate names may be trademarks or registered trademarks, and are used only for identification and explanation without intent to infringe.

ISBN: 978-1-032-95940-5 (hbk)
ISBN: 978-1-032-95939-9 (pbk)
ISBN: 978-1-003-58726-2 (ebk)

DOI: 10.4324/9781003587262

Typeset in Palatino
by Newgen Publishing UK

To the educators
who believe in the power of student voice.
To the students
who trust us with their poetry.
And to those who endeavor
to reimagine learning in stanzas.
Thank you for making education
a place where creativity thrives and
knowledge comes alive
in community.

Contents

Foreword xiv
Meet the Authors xvi

1 Humanizing Assessment Foundations and
   Framework 1
   Sarah J. Donovan

2 Using Visuals and Poetry Writing to Illuminate
   Student Learning 15
   Anna J. Small Roseboro

3 Poetic Pathways to Comprehension 49
   Sarah J. Donovan

4 Creative Inquiry: The Heart of Learning 99
   Barbara Edler

5 Unlocking Language: Poetry as a Tool for Vocabulary
   Study 140
   Gayle Sands

6 Summative Assessment: Demonstrating Learning
   as a Poetry Expo 183
   Kim Johnson

7 Reflecting Back and Moving Forward 211
   Anna J. Small Roseboro and Sarah J. Donovan

Foreword

As a former secondary English Language Arts (ELA) teacher and a current teacher educator, my journey has always been about finding and refining innovative teaching and assessment approaches. Over a decade ago, at a National Council of Teachers of English conference, I was introduced to Sarah Donovan and her "Ethical ELA" blog. That meeting was transformative for me as an educator. As I combed through her blog looking for recommendations on teaching poetry, I came across her article, "Student-Led Rehearsal Spaces for Collective Meaning in Poetry." This article opened my eyes to the power of poetry as not only a form of inquiry but also a form of assessment. Reading about Sarah's experiences guiding students through poetry as a means of exploring ideas and understanding, I was inspired to think differently about how students develop their knowledge and the ways in which educators assess knowledge. This shift in my thinking led to a shift in my teaching. Through the introduction of creating poetry to assess student learning in my own classroom, students' voices were lifted and doors to cross-discipline collaboration were opened.

As content area teachers know, the packed curriculum they are expected to "get through" can often leave little space for students to deepen their understanding of concepts and topics and demonstrate knowledge throughout the learning process. Furthermore, the opportunity to read and write like content area experts is often absent as well. However, as the authors of this book will show you, including the reading and writing of poetry in the curriculum can fill these gaps.

The opening chapter establishes the book's foundation and framework by defining "humanizing pedagogy" and illustrating how reading and creating poetry embodies this educational approach. Each subsequent chapter invites readers into various content area classrooms, showcasing how poetry fosters critical thinking, creative expression, and deeper engagement with subject matter. The authors provide anecdotal evidence of how reading and writing poetry empowers students to interpret images, explore language, build research skills and vocabulary, reflect on their learning, and express themselves creatively. They also demonstrate how poetry can be a valuable tool for assessing student understanding.

Importantly, the authors recognize that many teachers outside of ELA may have limited knowledge of poetry and how to teach it, which may lead to a hesitation to incorporate poetry into their curriculum. Teachers might wonder, *Where can I fit poetry into my curriculum? How can I use poetry to enhance student's understanding of content? How can writing poetry assess learning?* or even *What poems could I use?* The authors address these questions through detailed lesson plans, an extensive list of recommended poems and types, and cross-disciplinary lesson adaptations, providing content area teachers with practical guidance on integrating poetry into their curriculum.

Throughout this book, the authors show us that poetry can not only deepen students' connection to content but also help them find their place within it. By the end, you'll realize that poetry should not be limited to the ELA classroom; reading and writing poetry has the potential to transform student learning across all content areas.

Paula Greathouse, PhD
University of West Florida
*Adolescent Literature as a Complement
to the Content Area* – Book Series Editor

Meet the Authors

Sarah J. Donovan, Ph.D., is a celebrated author and educator dedicated to reshaping secondary English language arts through her roles as associate professor at Oklahoma State University and an active voice in poetry pedagogy, inclusive literacy, and youth literature. Her work centers on the power of literature and writing to build inclusive, humanizing spaces for students and teachers alike. Donovan is best known for her expertise in using poetry and young adult literature as tools for fostering community, nurturing identity, and enabling teachers and students to develop a curriculum that reflects human experiences.

With a Ph.D. in English from the University of Illinois, Chicago, Donovan's research introduced "Transactional Consciousness Theory," a framework for teaching complex topics like genocide through literature, helping students engage empathetically with difficult histories. She has since authored numerous academic and creative works, including articles in journals such as *Research in Teaching English*, *English Education*, *Teaching/Writing*, and *English Journal*. She co-authored books and chapters on writing pedagogy, trauma literacy, and teacher identity. Her publications reflect her commitment to anti-bias, anti-racist (ABAR) practices and the importance of giving voice to marginalized narratives in education. She and Eliza Ramirez won the Linda Rief Award for their article in *Voices from the Middle*.

Beyond her publications, Donovan is deeply invested in mentorship and collaboration. She actively supports undergraduate and graduate students and practicing teachers in their research and creative endeavors.

Donovan's reach extends to her work with the National Council of Teachers of English (NCTE) and the Assembly on Literature for Adolescents (ALAN), where she has served as a board member and columnist. She has received national recognition for her impact on teaching youth literature. She frequently presents at conferences, addressing themes such as poetry's role in education, supporting LGBTQ+ students, and developing inclusive pedagogies that challenge biases. Her workshops and presentations emphasize the need for ethical, empathetic teaching practices, and creative expression, making her a sought-after speaker and thought leader in English education.

An advocate for teacher-writers, Donovan founded initiatives like Ethical ELA, a website with free professional development. #VerseLove is an April event that provides teachers with supportive spaces to reflect and create through poetry. The #Verselove project won the 2024 Divergent Award. The Open Write is a monthly writing group that developed protocols to guide students in reading with empathy, understanding trauma, and fostering healing. Her recent book projects, including *90 Ways of Community* and *Words That Mend*, explore the therapeutic potential of poetry in educational settings and encourage teachers and students to write with authenticity and purpose.

Through her writing, mentorship, and public scholarship, Donovan continues to impact the field of secondary English education. Her work inspires educators to build classrooms that value each student's humanity, encourage resilience, and champion diverse voices. Her efforts to make literature a transformative experience position her as a leader in fostering inclusive, reflective learning environments that resonate deeply with both students and teachers.

Kim Johnson, EdD., is an accomplished educator, literacy specialist, and published author with over three decades of experience in education. Her career spans roles as a teacher at all levels from preschool through secondary grades, literacy coach, media specialist, literacy grant administrator, and district leader, demonstrating her unwavering commitment to fostering literacy and academic excellence.

Dr. Johnson holds a Doctorate in Teacher Leadership from Walden University, a Specialist's Degree in Education with an emphasis on Media and Instructional Technology from the

University of West Georgia, and a Master of Arts in Education with a focus on Literacy for Middle and Secondary Grades from Cambridge College. She earned her Bachelor of Arts in Early Childhood Education from the University of South Carolina.

Her foundational years in education included roles at Hilton Head International Baccalaureate Elementary School and Hilton Head Elementary School, where she contributed to writing curriculum for the IBPYP program at her school, piloted innovative teaching methods and several models for student-led conferences and presented at national conferences.

Johnson's classroom experience includes teaching at preschool, primary, elementary, middle, and secondary levels. She served as a teacher of gifted and general education students in reading, language arts, and social studies, earning recognition as Teacher of the Year at both the school and - wide levels.

She firmly believes in the power of collaboration between educators, administrators, and central office faculty to implement evidence-based literacy practices from Pre-K to Grade 12. She has spearheaded the development of innovative Literacy Labs designed to enhance student engagement and achievement. Her leadership extends to analyzing and addressing literacy data and delivering professional development to equip educators with effective strategies for maximizing learning. Additionally, she creates opportunities for community partners to offer literacy-based events to enhance the cultural fabric of literacy in her rural area.

Dr. Johnson is a prolific writer and speaker, having authored several publications, including her dissertation, *A Program Evaluation of the Document-Based Question Project*, and a humorous childhood memoir *Father Forgive Me: Confessions of a Southern Baptist Preacher's Kid*. She also worked with Dr. Sarah Donovan and others on Oklahoma State University's Oral History Project, focusing on writing poetry through Covid, and has contributed to various poetry anthologies. Her research and creative work explore topics such as collaborative writing, inquiry-based learning, and cross-curricular projects, with her articles featured in outlets like *Writers Who Care* and presentations delivered at prestigious forums, including the National Council of Teachers of English (NCTE) National Conventions and regional and state conferences. Most recently, she wrote as a contributing author for *Words that Mend: The Transformative Power of Writing Poetry for Teachers, Students, and Community Wellbeing*, A passionate advocate for inspiring life-long learning, Dr. Johnson's teaching philosophy emphasizes student choice and voice, collaborative inquiry, and real-world connections. Her work empowers both students and teachers to engage in reflective practices. She actively contributes to the teacher-writer community *Ethical ELA*, where she co-hosts writing events that inspire educators to incorporate poetry and other forms of writing into their classrooms.

Anna J. Small Roseboro, NBCT, is an award-winning educator, mentor, and author whose career spans more than five decades of teaching, writing, and advocating for diversity and equity in education.

A wife and mother, Anna earned a Bachelor's degree in Speech Communications and Secondary English Teaching Credentials from Wayne State University, followed by a Master of Arts in Curriculum Design from the University of California, San Diego. She is also a National Board-Certified Teacher and National Writing Project Fellow, whose expertise has influenced students and educators across the United States.

Anna began her teaching career in Detroit before moving on to roles in St. Louis, Rochester, Wilbraham, San Diego, and Grand Rapids. Her dedication to her craft led to teaching appointments at renowned institutions, including The Bishop's School in California, Grand Valley State University, and Calvin University in Michigan.

In addition to classroom teaching, Anna has excelled as a mentor and leader, chairing English departments, coaching speech and debate teams, and guiding aspiring teachers.

Her contributions extend far beyond her local classrooms. Anna served as president of the California Association of Teachers of English and chaired multiple committees for the National Council of Teachers of English, including initiatives to mentor Early-Career Educators of Color. She has been recognized with numerous honors, including the Distinguished Service Awards from CATE and NCTE, the MCTE Ray H. Lawson Award for Leadership, and the Classroom Excellence Award from the California Association of Teachers of English.

As an author, Anna has written extensively for educators, students, and readers of all ages.

Her books on teaching include *Empowering Learners: Teaching Different Genres and Texts to Diverse Student Bodies* (2023) (Co-author: Susan B. Steffel), *Planning with Purpose: A Handbook for New College Classroom Teachers* (2021) Co-author: Catherine A. Marschall); *Not Intimidating: Teaching Different Reading Genres to a Diverse Student Body* (2019), and *Getting Started: A Path to Success in Teaching English to Middle School Students and Beyond* (2018).

Anna's creative works demonstrate her versatility as a writer. Her poetry collection *Experience Poems and Pictures* (2019) and children's book *Rainbow Reminders* (2021) celebrate imagination and learning. Meanwhile, her novel series, *Two, One … Now Three: How Can That Be?* (2022) and *Choices, Choices? Chosen!* (2024) explores themes of resilience and identity.

In addition to her books, Anna has published numerous articles in respected journals such as *English Journal* and *Fine Lines*, addressing topics like culturally responsive teaching and innovative classroom strategies.

Her writing and leadership reflect her lifelong mission to empower learners and teachers in diverse communities.

Throughout her career, Anna has participated in initiatives that shape the future of education. She has served as a mentor for early-career educators through NCTE's Leadership Institute, contributed to teacher preparation guidelines, and presented at national and international conferences.

Today, Anna continues writing, mentoring, and advocating for educational excellence. She inspires educators and students worldwide, offering practical strategies and uplifting stories that emphasize the power of teaching and learning to transform lives.

Barbara Edler, M.A., began her career at a small rural school in northeast Iowa. She received her Masters from Western Illinois

University and her BA from Mount Mercy College, while continuing her education throughout her years as an educator, working with both students and mentoring pre-service teachers.

Today, she continues to tutor students in composition. After retiring from public school teaching in 2020, she worked part-time as a Composition instructor for both Iowa Wesleyan College and Kirkwood Community College.

As a high school English teacher and college composition teacher, she encouraged students to find their own voice, take risks, and consider various forms of presenting information. She coached students for Iowa High School Speech Association events for 30 years and has supported students with various competitions and activities including the Scholastic Writing Awards, National History Day, and Invent Iowa. Some of her fondest memories include directing spring plays at Oxford Junction High School and working with students to publish a literary magazine for several years at Keokuk High School.

Early in her career, she was deeply influenced by her experiences with the Iowa Writing Project which, at the time, was directed by James Davis. This program's philosophy centers on student learning and highly encourages teachers to write with their students to model their own approach to a writing task. Edler's IWP experience led her to work with David E. Wilson, and she contributed to his book *Attempting Change: Teachers Moving from Writing Project to Classroom Practice.*

In 2016, she returned to the University of Iowa to receive her Talented and Gifted Endorsement. During this time, she collaborated with her mentor, Diane Berner, and teacher, leader Natalie Ulloa to establish Keokuk High School as a STEM BEST school and received a $50,000 grant which was used to create a flexible and active learning space for all students and staff to enjoy. While working with gifted students, she was able to help many achieve personal learning goals and to receive significant scholarship opportunities.

Barbara has also written curricula for the state of Iowa and narratives for Pearson Education. Throughout the years she has presented a variety of speaking and writing topics for the Iowa

Council of Teachers of English and National Council of English Teachers conventions. Her poetry has been published in *Words that Mend: The Transformative Power of Writing Poetry for Teachers, Students, and Community Wellbeing*, *The Cities of the Plains: An Anthology of Iowa Artists and Poets*, and *Bridge the Distance: Teacher-Poets Writing to Bridge the Distance: An Oral History of COVID-19 in Poems*. Her work has also been published in editions of the *Grant Wood Country Chronicle* and *Lyrical Iowa*. Edler finds writing to be both healing and joyful.

Currently, she is the executive director of the Keokuk Art Center where she develops artistic events for adults and children. She is also the secretary of the Iowa Poetry Association and continues to challenge her writing chops by crafting poems using a variety of forms and by entering writing battles.

Gayle Sands, M.Ed., retired in 2020 after a fulfilling 27-year career as a middle school ELA teacher, where she dedicated herself to supporting struggling readers and writers. Anticipating a quiet life with her husband and numerous pets, she soon realized that retirement was not her calling. Embracing a new chapter, she took on the role of Professional Development School Liaison at McDaniel College, where she now mentors and oversees the in-school practicum experience for McDaniel's secondary education students in Carroll County Public Schools.

Throughout her career, Sands made significant contributions to her school and the county's educational system. She held key leadership roles including Team Leader, Chairperson of the School Improvement Team, and membership on both Carroll County Public School's Editorial Advisory Board and the Carroll County Superintendent's Advisory Committee. In addition to her many achievements, she devoted more than 15 years to crafting an English-Language Arts curriculum for Carroll County Middle Schools. She also contributed her expertise to developing a curriculum for the Maryland State Department of Education for several years. Sands's efforts earned her recognition as a three-time CCPS Outstanding Teacher finalist. She also served as Vice President of the Carroll County Reading Association and contributed as an active member of the CCPS Non-Traditional Learner Committee.

In 2003, she was asked to co-pilot a start-up initiative for an intervention team aimed at supporting incoming sixth graders at Northwest Middle School. Through the provision of additional instructional time for reading and math, coupled with a robust framework to foster student accountability and self-confidence, the team achieved remarkable outcomes. Students demonstrated dramatic improvements in reading and math skills, along with increased independence and self-belief. Many of these students eventually pursued higher education. The program's success led to its replication across the county.

As a result of her success, she was invited to help reorganize the county's alternative school program, aiming to enhance the academic content for students. She dedicated five rewarding and challenging years at the alternative school before returning to her home school as a Reading Resource Teacher and English Department Chair.

Sands' passion for words bloomed early. An avid reader from a young age, she found joy in diagramming sentences as a fourth grader and became the National Evening News Spelling Bee Champion for her county for four consecutive years. Sadly, she did not claim victory at the New York State Spelling Bee and her journey as a super-speller came to an end. However, her love for words did not. She began writing poetry in middle school and has continued to do so ever since. When she discovered Ethical ELA, she found a place to learn about and share her poetry.

Today, she shares her passion for education and language with her college students, regardless of their field of study. Through her coaching and encouragement, she strives to cultivate compassionate and skilled future teachers, hoping they will bring a touch of poetry into their own classrooms.

1

Humanizing Assessment Foundations and Framework

Sarah J. Donovan

What is Formative Assessment?

You already know what formative assessment is. You have been applying various strategies to find out what students know and can do throughout the school year. Maybe some of these examples sound familiar:

After your lesson on prime numbers, you ask your students to complete a worksheet. You may have several multiple-choice questions, such as: Which of the following numbers is a composite number? A. 2, B. 11, C. 27, D. 19. The worksheet may ask which one is a prime number or which series of numbers includes only composite numbers. You bolded the words to help with test-taking skills. You may have included a great table on the worksheet with one column of prime and one of composite numbers; you ask learners to decide which number does not belong in each column. What can you tell about your instruction and the student's learning from the results that you observe? What are your next steps for instruction, and for whom?

DOI: 10.4324/9781003587262-1

In Spanish class, you are teaching learners how to use the verb gustar. You have created a chart with images of activities and the Spanish word for that activity (e.g., two people dancing with the word bailar). You model the activity by saying, "Me llamo Sarah (My name is Sarah) y me gusta bailar (and I like to dance)." Then, each student practices with an elbow partner, or a peer seated nearby. You walk around, observing and listening to students. You feel good because a few minutes prior, most students did not know gustar or the words for verbs describing activities.

As you prepare for a unit on Juneteenth in History class, you use a template to assess formatively how much students know about source analysis. You hand out the template or post the Google form to your learning management system (Blackboard, Canvas, Google Classroom, etc.). The form allows you to see what students know about the source, the source's author, and the author's perspective based on word choice or sourcing. This formative pre-unit assessment lets you decide what to prioritize in your instruction.

Formative assessment is one of the most popular terms in school improvement. Still, if you came to teaching without a comprehensive teacher preparation program, you have yet to hear this term even though you already use this strategy to guide the next steps in your instruction.

Humanizing Assessment Practices

When we decided to include the word "humanizing" in the title of this book, we did so mainly to remind us (and you) to be conscious of the ways assessment and grading have traditionally focused on measurement and how, in talking about results and scores, we may find schools referring to students in terms of numbers or rankings ("on-level," "D-student," "high achiever," "underperforming") rather than their names, lives, and lived experiences.

Humanizing pedagogy means our practices honor and respect one's humanity and unique background. In our assignments and how we position students to demonstrate their learning, we are conscious of our students' agency and autonomy regarding social justice/injustice issues. We teach to enable the development of an individual's full human potential, drawing on the affordances of their age and youth culture, funds of knowledge, complete grammar systems, digital literacies, and intersectional identities. (See Figure 1.1.)

A humanizing pedagogy is an ongoing intentional practice of developing teaching and learning experiences that enable agency, a sense of coming not only to know content knowledge but also to *own* and be empowered by it. We see writing poetry as embodying this practice.

"An" Assessment vs Assessing

We, the authors in this book, have all mentored teachers by hosting student teachers in our classrooms, teaching in teacher preparation programs, observing teachers during their internships, and conducting education research across the stages of teachers' careers. We can say that the ways teachers and schools talk about assessment vary greatly, and we want to discuss at least two ways that will be relevant to understanding this book.

First, "assessment" is used to discuss an assignment. What assessment are you using? Assessment, sometimes, refers to the assignment and, sometimes, to the teacher's activity. As discussed above, the assessment might be a quiz on paper or a quiz in Kahoot, an online assessment digital platform. It might be an exit slip. In other words, assessment is what the student does to show they are progressing toward the learning goal.

Another way educators talk about assessment is by analyzing the assessment or assessing if or how students learned something. Teachers determine when they listen in on a group discussion about a story. The teacher assesses student comprehension or assesses if they have given clear instructions. A teacher might stop group work during a conversation to redirect their learning because the teacher "assessed" the instructions were unclear or there was some nuance in the concept that the teacher needed to clarify or re-teach.

Sometimes, the assessment comes after the teacher collects the quiz or exit slip. The teacher is deciphering how well the students do. Still, perhaps more importantly, the teacher is determining how practical their lesson was, how relevant the examples were, and how well they designed the "assessment" or assignment to show student learning. Full disclosure: We discovered during this assessment that the assignment we created was not as effective as we had hoped. For example, sometimes, our questions were worded poorly, or we failed to ask "how" or "why" a student selected a response. In other words, assessing is a lot like evaluating the effectiveness of the tool or assignment.

See how all this can get confusing? We hope that you see that, well, it is all assessment. We are constantly assessing, and that is good. We want to show how writing poetry as an assessment (assignment) and determining learning can be a healthy way of cultivating a classroom that values ongoing assessment. We hope that you and the students see that we need to be conscious about designing learning experiences that invite students to work with the content and language of the discipline to create meaning through their own lived experiences and ways of thinking. Poetry writing is an assessment and assigning poetry writing is a way of assessing.

Learning as a Reading Process

Much of learning across content areas is dependent upon some text. The text could be a textbook, article, primary source document, speech, video, slideshow, or lecture.

When we ask students to read informational texts, their attention tends to be focused on what they must do "after" the reading—the information they are supposed to remember, the solution to the problem, and the next steps they must take. Reading theorist Louise Rosenblatt names this as *efferent* reading—what you are doing now, perhaps. In contrast, in *aesthetic* reading, according to Rosenblatt, the reader is attending to what they are experiencing as they read, listen, and watch the text. The exact text, a page from your textbook, may be read either way. Students may be learning what causes a volcano to erupt (an efferent stance), or the class may turn their attention to imagining the aftermath of its eruption on villagers (an aesthetic stance).

The text's meaning depends on the reader and their stance or stance. A text—your lecture, slideshow, photograph, video, song, textbook, story—depends on a reader (student) to make sense of it and make meaning. The content can only have meaning if there is a transaction with a reader, listener, or viewer—in our case, a student. The reader brings to the text their past experiences and present personality. In your lesson, they get all their resources from memory, thought, and feeling. Moreover, they have a new experience. Rosenblatt calls this new experience a poem in the abstract sense, and we want to encourage educators to invite a physical poem to reflect this learning.

Doesn't that sound fantastic? Your students will come to your lesson on quadratic equations, your research on natural hazards, and Alexander Hamilton's speech as learning events that shape them as human beings (and, sometimes, all in the same day). It is no wonder that a quiz or exit slip might fail to capture this novel experience or meaning-making that each student is generating during your fantastic lesson. Have you considered that the lessons you give are not neutral? Is the assessment/assignment you offer not neutral? You might be missing out on some incredible meaning-making in that assessment/assignment you designed.

Teachers cannot see what all the circuits are doing, what images come up for students, what past lessons are firing, and what new connections are being built. We know from our experiences that writing a poem creates learning and is an opportunity to capture that meaning-making experience.

Meaning-making is where those formative assessments come in, but can you see the meaning-making process of each student, or has the worksheet constrained this process to some degree? Has the worksheet kept the student from playing with content, moving language, adding their own experiences, and shaping the words into new phrases? What we mean, here, is that, with formative assessments, you are asking students to make a new text for you to interpret then or assess. Get it? Yes, when you read the text the student made for you, it becomes another poem, another event in the transaction between you and the text. You marshal your resources and make meaning from what the student has created.

Here is the question (and why we wrote this book): What sort of text do you need from the students to engage you in meaning-making? Put another way, the students are making a text for you when you ask them to take a quiz or complete an exit slip. Is that the best we can ask of our students? What sort of formative assessment will help you understand the meaning-making process of your students and allow you to reciprocate in another transaction (your next lesson)? How can you keep the circuit of meaning alive—the poem circuit between you/your text and the student/text and the student's text/you, and so on?

After a lesson, most teachers want to know what students learned from our lecture, the video, the textbook, the article, or the discussion. Assessment has been missing the poem—the whole live processing circuit where meaning-making and learning happen. Traditional assessments of quizzes, 3-2-1, and one-sentence summaries do not uncover that for us. We want to know the past learning and lived experiences students draw on and their present state, interests, and preoccupations in transacting with the content.

We may be asking for an "answer," but we, perhaps, should be more interested in the active process lived through during the students "reading" of the lesson. We may ask students to write an active-reading journal or take notes- this is great. But then what after? How are students synthesizing, processing, and reworking ideas to learn more deeply? What sort of text can students create in their formative assessment to allow for the creation of another text? What new events can we offer students for ongoing meaning-making? What "texts" can they create to add more live circuits to our classrooms?

Learning as a Writing Process

Writing to learn or writing across the curriculum (WAC) is nothing new, but teachers only sometimes engage students in writing with intentionality. Teachers may use writing to activate prior knowledge with a prompt at the beginning of a lesson. Sometimes, teachers ask students to write a K-W-L activity: **write what you know, what you want to know, and what you learned**. Generally, writing-to-learn activities are short, low-stakes assignments that help students think about the content or ideas somebody presented or is about to present. They tend to take up little time, and teachers tend to spend less time assessing them.

We and other educator-scholars believe that writing is underutilized in classrooms even though it promotes critical thinking, such as synthesizing prior experiences and new knowledge. Individuals also use writing to inform, instruct, persuade, and tell stories. Of course, after a lesson, we want to find out what the students learned, and writing can show this, but still, only some educators carve time for students to write in content areas beyond language arts. Students can use writing to order and present their learning experience; they can use language to show but also to discover and uncover, and, in doing so, show new learning that even the teacher could not have anticipated.

Writing to learn nurtures an ability to think, rationalize, and reason. Students draw on skills to summarize, pose problems, clarify, plan, discover, define, and organize. So much cognitive work happens when students write. This book calls for teachers to use writing as an assessment—the assignment—and in assessing learning.

Why Poetry?

We know that teacher preparation programs do not often include a teaching writing course for language arts and certainly not for other content areas. While the National Writing Project has sites nationwide to support teacher-writers in developing authentic writing instruction, only some schools offer teachers ongoing professional development for writing instruction, even though writing is part of every content area.

In this book, poetry is a way to promote reading and writing to learn because it is a concentrated form with endless possibilities that take little time to create, share, or grade. Poetry brings efferent and aesthetic experiences and meaning-making to create a new text for the learner, their peers, and the teacher. The poem becomes evidence of learning and a new text that extends learning to others who experience the poem.

Writing poetry enables learners to expand content area language skills as they compose poetry within the discourse of historians, mathematicians, and scientists. For example, student poets use line breaks and stanzas to organize ideas rather than paragraphs. They draw on phrasing to show patterns within the content area. Moreover, learners must decide what is essential, as most poems prefer an economy of words.

The chapters that follow show how the poetry form can illuminate these decisions. For example, consider an acrostic poem to capture the essential facts of a war. Consider a haiku to express the turn or implication of a problem. Consider a pantoum to show the themes of a play. How about a list poem to show the steps to analyze a line graph? If you do not recall these poetic forms, no worries; we will show you in the following chapters, where we define and describe various poetic structures. You will see what you need to proceed and succeed.

How to Use This Book

The subject matter or grade levels represented differ from yours as you read. Please do not skim over or disconnect from these sections, as irrelevant to your work. The ideas still apply to you and can be easily adapted with little effort, such as the teacher learning new ways to assess learning or refining their practice. You are the content expert here, and we offer ways to bring students into deep thinking about your content so that they can engage in deep meaning-making beyond recalling or repeating your lecture or video lesson.

We, the colleagues writing this book, hope you adopt or adapt the ideas offered here. We have benefitted from teachers doing just that. We tried these lessons in multiple content areas and across many schools and tweaked our work with their formative feedback. The figure "Assessment through Writing Poetry Framework" concisely offers a snapshot of the affordances of writing poetry and shows how concepts grounded in humanizing English language arts teacher preparation principles can be engaged in your instructional practice (see Figure 1.1).

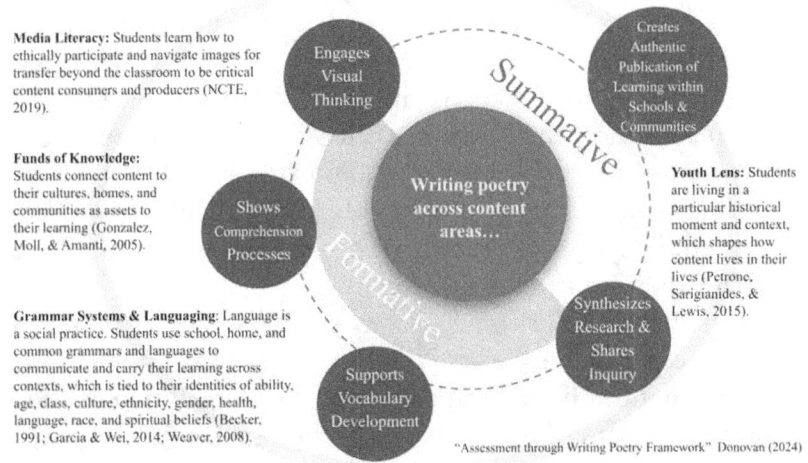

FIGURE 1.1 Assessment through writing poetry framework.

Focusing on grades 6-12, we anchor our work in a Youth Lens (Petrone et al., 2014). Students live in a particular historical moment and context, shaping how content lives in their lives and adolescence. Our students are content consumers living many of their lives on social media, and they are content creators, which means they are informing media feeds of others and have a digital reach beyond their physical and social groups and family. A Youth Lens means we know that students have the capacity to do incredible things, and writing poetry in class offers time and space for students to have agency in making meaning with content learning.

Writing poetry engages visual thinking. What media literacy means is ever-changing as students engage with dynamic feeds of content streaming. We connect visual thinking and writing poetry to support students in ethically participating in and navigating images for transfer beyond the classroom so that they can be critical media consumers and producers (NCTE, 2019). We see students as shaped by and capable of shaping these media feeds. As students interact with new content, they connect it with their cultures, homes, and communities, all assets to their learning (Gonzales et al., 2005). These connections humanize our classrooms, making learning dynamic.

Every content area depends on grammar systems (Weaver, 2008) and languaging (Becker, 1991; Garcia & Wei, 2014) to convey and uncover content. Language is a social practice. Students use school, home, and ordinary grammar and languaging to communicate and carry their learning across contexts. In every context, students bring their identities and experiences living those identities in this sociopolitical climate. Their ability, age, class, culture, ethnicity, gender, sexuality, health, languages, race, and spiritual beliefs inform their learning.

Content-specific learning allows students to participate in discourse communities with you—speaking like a scientist as they learn natural hazards and reading like a historian as they consider the origin of primary source photographs. The various content discourses they navigate daily are integrated into their grammar systems and languaging practices as students move across various digital, physical, and temporal contexts of their lives.

Chapter Overviews

Chapter 2 focuses on using poetry as a creative tool for making meaning from and with images. Anna J. Small Roseboro emphasizes the importance of engaging students in poetry writing to enhance their understanding of historical events. The veteran educator highlights the connection between poetry and various content areas, such as science, geography, and social studies, emphasizing the value of creative and critical thinking.

The chapter outlines a step-by-step approach to teaching poetry to make meaning of images (e.g., infographics, photographs, art), offering examples of different types of poems, including pantoum, acrostic, and elegy. The pantoum poem structure, where lines are repeated and expanded upon, is used to explore historical facts and events. The acrostic poem encourages students to answer critical questions about historical figures or events using the letters of a chosen name or place. Lastly, the elegy poem commemorates significant individuals from history and can be designed to connect students to their cultural heritage. Overall, Anna underscores the potential of poetry to engage students with image-based texts to promote a deeper understanding of historical events and encourage creative expression in the context of content-based learning as it relates to diversity, inclusion, and equity.

Chapter 3 demonstrates how poetry can be a powerful tool for comprehension. Sarah J. Donovan offers one Spanish lesson to invite students to craft poems about influential writers, exploring how historical, social, and cultural events shaped these figures. While designed for Spanish teachers, most content area educators can adapt this lesson plan for any subject by replacing Spanish writers with influential historical figures, scientists, artists, and more.

The chapter also introduces mentor text poems as an effective alternative to traditional reports, fostering creative expression and critical thinking. Sarah includes a lesson on environmental science, particularly natural hazards and their effects on human activity. It aligns with most 2020 state learning standards, emphasizing students' ability to construct explanations based on natural resources, hazards, and climate change evidence. Inspired by George Ella Lyon's "Where I'm From" poems, students write poems about the causes and impacts of their selected geological hazards, fostering comprehension and personal reflection. Finally, considering maths, students use their understanding of discrete and continuous data to compose poems reflecting the influence of their surroundings on their identity and behavior. This creative exercise prompts students to consider how data shapes graphs and how interpretation varies across different graphs. The chapter underscores peer interaction and healthy assessment and grading practices while nurturing an inclusive learning community.

In Chapter 4, Barbara Edler emphasizes the significance of supporting student learning through inquiry. Barbara highlights the role of review and analysis in building prior knowledge and fostering students' engagement. The chapter also discusses strategies for sparking students' interest, including visuals, videos, and questionnaires. It delves into teaching strategic skills through a captivating unit on the Civil Rights Movement, encouraging students to conduct independent research and share their findings creatively. The chapter introduces three lessons, each involving inquiry and free verse poetry—Twenty Questions, News and New, and Voices from the Past—to deepen students' understanding and encourage self-assessment, ultimately preparing them for a successful future. She shares reflections on her visits to three high school classrooms: First Aid, Advanced Science, and Freshman English, to demonstrate how these strategies can be implemented.

In Chapter 5, Gayle Sands tackles the challenge of engaging students in meaningful language and vocabulary development. She demonstrates how poetry can support teachers in introducing and assessing students' understanding of academic content language. Gayle shares a story of a diverse 6th-grade science class as they review vocabulary terms for a test. Drawing on research, Gayle uncovers how the conventional practices of introducing essential vocabulary words from the textbook or testing on vocabulary lists can fail to connect with students' funds of knowledge and interests. Gayle proposes an innovative poetry approach that motivates educators to teach subject-specific vocabulary in two poetic forms: the Sevenling and Hay(na)ku. This method aims to make vocabulary learning enjoyable and expand students' understanding as a review practice. The chapter suggests various interactive activities, provides a practical process for implementing the lessons, and offers a grading rubric with ethical support for evaluating and celebrating students' content-based poetry.

In Chapter 6, Kim Johnson showcases a successful and adaptable summative assessment strategy using a Humanities Pathway program in a high school in Georgia. The program focuses on the United Nations Sustainable Goals, with this specific unit addressing the use of various poetry forms to show what students are learning about the impact of genocide in different areas of our world. Kim describes how poetry is integrated into the curriculum, allowing students to express their understanding and emotions related to the subject.

The chapter begins with background information about the program and its mission, highlighting the use of interest-based elective classes to engage students. She explains how each unit is centered around a UN Goal and includes book clubs and discussions to explore the topic. Kim offers tips for teachers to enhance the poetry writing experience, such as using decorative paper and videos to create a visually appealing and interactive display of student poems during the Student Learning Expo. The chapter concludes with snapshots from the Expo event, showcasing how students displayed their poems, engaged with stakeholders, and shared their insights. Overall, this chapter highlights an innovative and emotionally engaging approach to teaching a challenging topic like genocide, using poetry as a means for students to express their understanding and contribute to meaningful conversations.

Together, we have crafted a book that shows educators how to use poetry for formative assessment across the content areas. Whether the text teachers want students to read is from a Calculus textbook, a Psychology article, a Civil Rights lecture slideshow, a video explanation on Agronomy, or primary source photography in Journalism, writing poetry can be a way learners make meaning, a pathway to learning that values the students' lived experiences and celebrates the making of new texts (poetry) as evidence of learning and insight.

Educators must adapt to meet their students' changing needs and interests in an increasingly efficiency-focused age. With AI, teachers are concerned about the authenticity of writing. With state dyslexia policies, teachers are looking for new ways to differentiate. With the increase in trauma-sensitive teacher training, teachers wonder how to integrate content and social-emotional support. With content area experts stepping in to fill emergency positions, teachers recognize that content knowledge needs pedagogical knowing.

We believe the craft of poetry helps humanize the art of expression, reflection, and analysis (even if poetry standards are not explicit in many state standards). The book explores how poetry can present itself as a short, creative assessment tool that helps teachers see, determine, and measure what students know and can do while offering students space to make new meaning in their original poetry. Let us get started.

References

Becker, A. L. (1991). Language and languaging. *Language and Communication, 11,* 33–35.

Garcia, O., & Wei, L. (2014). *Translanguaging: Language, bilingualism and education.* Palgrave Macmillan.

González, N., Moll, L., & Amanti, C. (Eds.). (2005). *Funds of knowledge: Theorizing practices in households, communities, and classrooms.* Erlbaum.

NCTE, National Council of Teachers of English. (2019, November 7). NCTE's definition of literacy in a digital age. *National Council of Teachers of English.* https://ncte.org/statement/nctes-definition-literacy-digital-age/

Petrone, R., Sarigianides, S. T., & Lewis, M. A. (2014). The youth lens: Analyzing adolescence/ts in literary texts. *Journal of Literacy Research, 46*(4), 506–533.

Weaver, C. (2008). *Grammar to enrich and enhance writing.* Heinemann.

2

Using Visuals and Poetry Writing to Illuminate Student Learning

Anna J. Small Roseboro

> Tell me and I forget; teach me and I may remember; involve me and I learn.
> ~Benjamin Franklin

You have just taught an incredibly challenging unit to students in history, geography, or social studies. The long holiday break is coming. The learners will be restless, but you know that a mere week after their return, a summative exam is scheduled. Knowing what students have learned so far will help you plan a unit review that can begin before the holiday because such a guided student choice assignment can help them focus on what they know and what they need to learn.

Using one or more poetic strategies can help measure student learning and discover gaps in their understanding. Ideas in this chapter can help. You will find sample assignments, steps for implementing them as homework, and interactive in-class activities, along with a sample grading rubric that serves as a tool to measure how students' poetry shows what they know about unit content. You can verbalize activities goals and allow students to make choices.

Poetry is a genre of writing designed to capture ideas, thoughts, and experiences in just a few carefully selected words but need not have a specific rhyme or rhythm pattern. Learners may need to be more familiar with how to write poetry when they begin secondary education. However, your modeling poetry writing of the forms you assign should suffice, because you have tried them beforehand or simply provided examples. Also, what students write for this activity can take less time for teachers to read as multiple pages of descriptive, expository, or argumentative essays in some core content area classes.

Student-produced poetry may assume the role of diagnostic, formative, or summative assessment of content unit learning. Assigning learners to write poetry about their learning in any content area is a research-based strategy for inspiring students to think deeply about their learning. Cognitive skills of summarizing, synthesizing, analyzing, comprehension, and comparison can all be measured when reading students' poetry (McWhorter & Bullion-Mears, 2015). In short, poetry writing in history, geography, social studies, and other content area classrooms is a learner and teacher-centric exercise.

Teachers in the content areas can identify learning goals, discover alternative ways to assess students' learning, and then find different guides to design homework and in-class activities. Educators who teach history, for example, strive to implement practices that use such time efficiently and effectively, providing opportunities for students to produce evidence of their learning and revealing learning gaps in their knowledge of a historical period: the people, specific places, and identifiable events. A reliable assessment offered here entails using poetry to respond to graphics, photos, or paintings created to document or reflect those people, places, and events of a target historical period.

Writing poetry about pictures to experience artwork dates back to antiquity. The Greek term Ekphrastic has come to be defined as poems written about works of art. Students may get a charge out of knowing they are not doing something new but actually are continuing an activity older than most of the history they are studying with their teacher. As a result, teachers can explain how writing poetry has historical meaning for the era under learner investigation.

What stands out in research about using poetry for teaching middle and high school content is that poetry writing is a reliable writing-to-learn strategy. McWhorter and Bullion-Mears (2015) offer such insight:

> …poetry, because of its versatility, flexibility, and diversity of formats, provides an ideal link between content area concepts and writing to learn. Writing poetry helps students develop their abilities to record descriptions and visualize ideas, thus reinforcing concepts….
>
> (p. 46)

> Writing to learn has gained prominence in content-area literacy circles, where the process of journal writing, quick writes, possible sentences, cubing, composing poetry, and other strategies puts students in the driver's seat of their own learning.
>
> (Bean et al., 2011)

Learners "…filter [or]…sift and examine concepts and see how these sometimes-obscure notions…connect with their lives" (Bean et al., 2011, p. 272). Content areas of history and science may, at times, feel out of reach for learners. History can be viewed with temporal dissonance. Science can be seen as ontologically or epistemologically murky. Bean, Readence, and Balwin say that writing to learn bucks challenges temporal dissonance and ontological or epistemological misunderstandings of content area learning. In sum, Bean, Readence, and Baldwin maintain that "writing-to-learn activities initiate students to various methods for using writing to explore and integrate ideas arising from a content area" (p. 272). Poetry, you see, can be viewed as a pedagogical strategy for content area teaching and information gathering that works well when there is a need to discover the degree to which learning will, is, or has occurred.

As you consider ways to adapt the strategies in this chapter, consider ways the lessons can

- Be inviting and vigorous.
- Help students connect their lives to the topics.
- Challenge students to think deeply, critically, and broadly.
- Help the students to write clearly, correctly, and creatively.
- Encourage students to work independently, in pairs, triads, groups, or as a whole class, as will work best for each particular kind of poetry writing.
- Expand their understanding of themselves and their world.
- Develop ways for students to express themselves using a variety of poetic styles and genres, knowing the goal is to inspire deep thinking.
- Use digital technology effectively for research, writing, and communication.
- Reflect a healthy balance of structure and choice.

Collaborating in the Humanities

I came to this thinking of using poetry as a formative assessment with several years of experience as a classroom teacher, English Department Chair at a 7-12 school, and director of summer sessions at a school that had several cross-curricular activities including a full-fledged Humanities program for our eighth graders and strong interdisciplinary assignments for students in other grades. In English, we often selected a piece of literature set in or described events in the historical period students were studying in History or about topics in Science and Math.

Consider assigning various genres of poetry in Math and Science classes. One teacher posted photos of people from various cultures and races for whom knowledge of math is critical to success in their careers. This teacher would invite students to write letters to these historical personages. Today, this teacher, who field tested this theory while I was researching for my master's degree, would be advised to offer poetry writing as an option with letter writing. I'd probably recommend the acrostic, which I will describe later. This option would invite students to use the name of the person in the picture and write words or phrases about the math that begin with letters of that person's name. More on that later.

More and more, I suggest writing-to-learn activities that can be written as poems where students show what they are learning and how they can use recently taught math concepts in their daily lives. Remember, we teachers learn when we see what our students write. Consider offering poems that include certain combinations of numbers as choices. For example, haiku poetry is structured as 5/7/5: five syllables or words for the first and third lines and seven syllables or words in the middle line.

History and social studies teachers could invite students to consider the kinds of math students are studying that would be helpful for people living during critical historical events. For example, computing distances, figuring budgets using different currencies, and constructing homes and buildings. This idea of integrating various kinds of writing in the content areas is confirmed by Bean et al. (2017):

> …in classes where students write…, they feel like they are in the driver's seat…writing becomes a powerful vehicle for guiding students' learning—a filter through which they can sift and examine concepts and see how these sometimes obscure notions that connect with their lives.
> (p.272)

As you invite students to show in their poetry writing what they know about the people, places, and events, using the skills they are honing in other classes, you are reinforcing that learning as you discover what they know and are able to do in the course you teach and in content areas across the curricula. This purposeful collaboration reinforces learning in all areas.

Cross-curricular influences may be as specific or tangential as seen in the Art Departments where I used to teach. The art teachers would have students view, and then model art similar to that created by artists living in the historical setting the students in different grades were studying. For example, one year may be medieval history; another year, world history; another United States or European History.

Along the same pattern, music teachers may choose songs written about or performed by musicians in a specific historical period. Instrumental music teachers may invite students to play songs on instruments invented or made popular during a target historical period or by people of different cultures as related in the social studies text or selected fiction or nonfiction being read in English.

Colleagues in other arts did the same. The hands-on art department often chose to be guided by the historical people, places, and events students studied in social studies and history classes. Students would practice creating art in different mediums and with different materials based on the history they were studying. Our drama teacher chose to stage one-act plays that reflect what students have been studying in science.

One year, our ninth graders wrote one-act plays based on modern settings for Roman, Greek, and African myths about what the students were studying in science. We English teachers submitted class-selected "best of the bunch" to the drama department, which staged some of these student-written plays. Triple dipping into three departments further reinforced what students had, were, or would be learning.

In English, while students were studying ancient history in their Social Studies classes, we in the English Department were reading a middle school version of *The Canterbury Tales*. We assigned students to model the patterns they discovered in Geoffrey Chaucer's writing and write about a current trip they'd take that included the who, what, when, where, why, and how elements.

You could have students write poems using names, terms, and phrases important to their understanding of the historical time you are studying. Consider the pantoum, acrostic, and elegy, three genres I'll describe later in the sample lesson in the coming pages. Each of these poetry forms adapts easily for your purposes of measuring learning by reading student-drafted poetry. The key word here is "drafted." For purposes of formative assessment, the goal is to see what students know about the topic. Revisions and refinements in form can come later. Consider the styles and structures as measuring cups into which students pour their learning in an organized fashion.

Exploring Other Cultures, Religions, and Experiences

At a school with few students of African American descent, for several years, our drama teacher celebrated Black History Month by staging plays written by Black dramatists. Among those challenging our non-Black actors and actors was *For Colored Girls Only* (1976), adapted from a choral poem by Ntozake Shange, and another year, *Colored People's Time* (1983), a series of vignettes by Leslie Lee. For the drama students, learning the history and assuming the persona of "the other" proved to be a valuable learning experience offered by the drama teacher.

In fact, the challenge of being Black, even as performers on stage, was so difficult for some of the students that our drama teacher postponed presenting the play publicly until late Spring. The students took nearly three months to reflect on the reality of the historical periods and sense what the characters experienced so the student actors could portray the characters authentically.

Thankfully, the drama teachers considered the preparation important and thus rescheduled the performance once the students were ready. As you nurture safe spaces for your students to have comparable experiences, invite your learners to write poetry about pictures you show, but in the voice of people and cultures, ages, and regions different from that of the student writers.

Several of the assignments our school team designed included viewing and creating artistic depictions of what students were reading and then describing them in various genres. Poetry became one of my favorites. According to the Houghton-Mifflin College Dictionary (1996), poetry as

> a composition designed to convey a vivid and imaginative sense of experience, especially by the use of condensed language chosen for its sound and suggestive power, as well as for its meaning, and by using such literary techniques as structured meter, natural cadence, rhyme, or metaphor.

Because students' poetry can but need not have a specific structured meter or rhyme patterns, being free of those restrictions seems to ease the task for many of our students. The condensed language chosen for its meaning reveals so much about what students know and can do with the content they are learning in any study area. For other students, writing in the rhythm they hear in the songs of their faith or those they listen to on their tablets and cell phones makes writing poetry about what they are learning such a charge. Yes, charge. The rhythms get them going. The students feel the beats and get to writing.

As you continue reading, note ways my suggestions for you to incorporate writing poetry as an assessment tool are built on solid ground to incorporate diversity, inclusion, justice, and equity themes directly or subtly. So far, you have seen specific examples of interdisciplinary applications. When our eighth graders were studying Science in the English Department, we read myths from different cultures that attempted to explain natural phenomena in different geographic regions. The myths we explored included the traditional Greek and Roman stories about creation from Scandinavian, African, and Asian cultural groups.

When our juniors studied American History, they were encouraged to write about the social, economic, and political events that may have influenced the literature we were reading in English. For example, once students studied the Civil Rights Movement, we would read *Invisible Man* by James W. Ellison in our regular, honors, and AP English classes. When students read about the Vietnam War, they read *Monkey Bridge* by Lan Cao.

When students studied the Women's Rights Movement, we read *The Handmaid's Tale* by Margaret Atwood as a class. Further, we encouraged students to notice the similarities in English words that may have come into this language from the languages spoken in other countries.

As you collaborate with colleagues across the content areas, you, too, will find clever ways to have students incorporate into your assignments what they are learning in other courses and write interesting poems that show their burgeoning cache of knowledge and skills.

Learning by Looking

Even if your pre-service training or prior study of pedagogy did not include work regarding Multiple Intelligences made famous at the turn of the century in writing by Howard Gardner or with the VARK model that describes for us four types of learners: visual, auditory, kinesthetic, and reading/writing, you likely have noticed these styles or models among the students you now teach.

The following sample lessons include components that help reach three of these four learning styles: visual, auditory, and reading/writing. You will be encouraged to use and invite students to bring photos and artwork of persons, places, and events about the content learning you wish to assess. If nothing more, you will tap into one or more learning styles researchers say students have.

When visual learners see what they are being taught graphically, the message is received and remembered. The graphics may be charts, graphs, and maps. They also may be photos and works of art. Consider the impact of roadside billboards and murals used for advertisement. One of the reasons picture books are such powerful tools for use in middle and high school is that the drawings and colors used help relay the messages sent by the authors and publishers. The photos and artwork for this lesson can be accessed easily from the Library of Congress Archives (www.loc.gov/photos/collections/), and most of those photos, prints, and drawings are public domain, so there should be no issues related to fair use or copyrights.

The assignment also invites you to have students share their poems aloud, informally in small groups, or more formally as a presentation to the whole class. But, since the primary purpose of this particular lesson is to measure specific content learning, there need not be a formal presentation to be an efficient and effective use of class time. If, however, you decide to include oral presentations, you will find a simple rubric and feedback chart at this link of my website: *Teaching to Inspire* (https://teachingenglishlanguagearts.com/organizing-a-week-of-speeches/)

There, you will find a chart for organizing a week of speeches and a guide for students to provide feedback to their peers.

Here is a sample two- to three-day assignment for measuring student understanding of a specific historical period. It includes homework searches, in-class writing, and reflection.

1. For homework, give students links to pictures of the people, places, or events just studied. Consider the Library of Congress site with prints and pictures (www.loc.gov/collections/).
2. Then, the next day, you show students how to write a group pantoum poem in class. This means you will have explored this style and written one yourself. Then, after writing a class poem, give students the choice of writing an acrostic poem, an elegy, or a pantoum poem about their choice of these combinations:
   a. A person/group and an event
   b. A person/group in a specific place
   c. An event/incident in a specific place

Each poem should be written to show what students know about the target historical period's WHO, WHAT, WHEN, WHERE, WHY, and HOW. In doing so, learners must identify key facts about the content covered in class.

On the optional third day, invite students to read the poetry of their classmates and rate that writing or performance for content, not structural correctness. Of course, listeners and viewers are likely to rate the poems that reflect the creative use of poetry techniques, too. But those techniques can be optional in the rubric you provide for the students.

Assigning in-class writing will soon reveal to you what our collaborative team has observed. Students respond to these kinds of writing-to-learn assignments by paying closer attention to their textbook reading and in-class activities because they know they will be asked to articulate their understanding in their own words. Soon, you will begin to see more evidence of students as they begin to

- ♦ Focus on their assignments and performances;
- ♦ Analyze reasons for their success or failure in the subject;
- ♦ Reflect on what they read in their text and experience in the class;
- ♦ Verbalize more comfortably in written and oral form with you and their classmates;
- ♦ Collaborate more confidently because they already have begun thinking and finding words to express themselves precisely.

Of course, none of these is isolated. A student may focus and analyze during a reflection on pictures, maps, photos, and artwork. They may verbalize during a collaborative situation or oral presentation. Your goal as the teacher is to understand and implement class assignments that reflect humane ways to increase learning for you all.

Sample Lesson - History: The Northern Migration in the United States

A lesson on the Northern Migration in the United States exemplifies how to employ poetry writing to show what students have learned and how effectively you have taught about a significant historical phenomenon. Imagine having just completed a unit on the political events of the early 20th century between the World Wars. Consider the Harlem Renaissance years. One major event during those same years is the Northern Migration. Invite students to examine the artwork produced during and about that historical period. Invite them to consider the social, economic, and political events that spurred the art production. Alternatively, you may rely on photos from the Library of Congress resources mentioned above.

Older students may already be familiar with the acronym and the SEPs of social, economic, and political events that may be revealed or reflected in the fiction already read in class. However, as a history, geography, or social studies educator, one must underscore that fictional poetry written by students in fact-based content area learning spaces is meant to communicate knowledge about nonfictional events creatively.

Gorrell and Colflax (2012) observe that poetry teaching in the science classroom, which, like history, geography, and social studies, rests on non-fictional phenomena, results in "imaginative… responses."

The classroom atmosphere's active, hands-on, collaborative nature motivates students to write inspired poems, and students who have never before written poetry can become excited, engaged, and productive. The descriptive techniques shared by science and poetry allow for creative, critical, and metaphoric thinking that is valuable for teaching in both areas and offers new ways of thinking and writing about the natural world. (Gorrell & Colfax, 2012).

A subtle, underlying assumption in Gorrell and Colfax's thinking centers on engagement (Januchowski-Hartley et al., 2018). The interplay between poetry and science allows learners to view straightforward facts "about the natural world" from various perspectives that may not have otherwise emerged in learner thinking.

Learners often become critical of and excited about science by writing poetically about science itself. The same can be said about history, geography, and social studies. We learn this to be true when we invite students to write in the persona (as a person or character) from the historical period, place, or event they are studying in our classes. Biopoems can take many forms and be created on virtually any topic across content areas. Biopoems are particularly applicable to biographies but are very versatile as a creative way of writing to inform.

Completing a formative assessment task of poetry writing in a single class period of fifty minutes or so requires assigning as homework the task of viewing selected websites and the students coming to the next class with their choice of two pictures or graphic depictions each: persons, places, events from the unit of study. You decide whether or not to use class time for these photo searches since it is vital for students to have their chosen photo to view while drafting their poems.

Learner searches will be reviews, and their choices will be reflections. Students generally spend more time looking for what to bring to class when they choose which to bring from the approved sources than they would if they are limited to pre-assigned images of the persons, places, and events under consideration for poetry writing (Figure 2.1).

FIGURE 2.1 Public Domain Photo of Southern Family Packed and Ready for Northern Migration.

In class, have printed handouts or projected them on a screen for all to view for each step of the assignment. Seeing, reading, and hearing help students maintain focus. Then, you proceed to model the steps of poetry writing for a critical event that students may still need to understand. McWhorter and Bullion-Mears (2015) posit that "teachers…need to model the metacognitive and physical acts of writing directly to demonstrate their processing as they write about content concepts" (p. 46). Accordingly, write a pantoum poem with your learners that usually takes about 15 minutes to draft. Then, assign them to write an elegy or acrostic poem on their own based on one of the pictures they have chosen themselves.

The pedagogical approach described by Fisher and Frey in *Better Learning Through Structured Teaching* (2021) is what educationists dub the gradual release of responsibility, where the teacher offers concrete scaffolded learning experiences that bring about a learner's ability to carry out a task independently. Pulling from the gradual release idea will help when using poetry as a tool for history, geography, or social studies learning, in part because poetry writing is not a common learning task in such content-area classrooms.

Poem: Pantoum

A pantoum poem begins with four lines about a general topic or a unit of study in a particular content area. Typically, a line of poetry is seven to ten words. As previously mentioned, there is no need for rhyme or rhythm. Pantoum is a pattern poem of eight original lines, and then each original line is repeated in a specific order. One must practice writing pantoums before demonstrating how to create them in class so learners can follow suit. So, plan to draft your own poems, sampling each of the styles you offer as choices for student writing. Doing so will help you understand the thinking and the time it may take for your students to complete these drafts successfully. Refrain from stressing about punctuation at this point in the process. The goal is to discover what students know now and need to know soon.

To prepare for this in-class poetry writing lesson, consider assigning students to randomly structured groups of three or four and asking them to brainstorm and write as many historical facts about the northern migration as possible. Then, once the class begins writing the pantoum poem together, merge that list for all students to view. The goal is to get the facts up there so all can see, reflect, appraise, comment, and move on. See Figure 2.2, a worksheet for structuring the pantoum poem.

In the case of the Northern Migration, display these lines or your choice of facts about the historical era on the screen so students can see them.

Multiple concurrent events occurred between the World Wars:

1. People of color move north from segregated Southern states.
2. African Americans migrate from the rural south to the urban north.
3. Many groups seek higher income and access to better schooling.
4. Mexican Americans move north, often for better farm jobs.

After writing out the poem's first four lines, proceed to write the next four-line stanza. To do so, copy lines two and four of the poem's first stanza to become lines five and seven of the poem's second stanza and then invite students to write lines six and eight, which are expansions of the previous lines and become lines five and seven.

5. African Americans migrate from the rural south to the urban north.
6. (Student words that expand or explain the previous line.)
7. Mexican Americans move north, often for better farm jobs.
8. (Student words that expand or explain the previous line.)

Invite student volunteers to expand the thoughts of lines five and seven with facts they know already or were generated during the small group brainstorming sessions. When needed, classmates should substantiate the facts of their peers. The following procedure in modeling poem writing in a history class is to copy lines six and eight of the second stanza of a teacher-led poem onto lines nine and eleven of the third stanza. Then, once again, invite student volunteers to extend their knowledge of lines nine and eleven onto lines ten and twelve, which are two lines with facts about the Northern Migration unit.

9. ____Copy to repeat line six._____
___
10. (Student words that expand or explain the previous line.)____
11 Copy to repeat line eight._____
12. (Student words that expand or explain the previous line.)____

The final, four-line stanza of a pantoum poem repeats the lines of the poem in the following order:

13. (7)_____
14. (3) _ Many groups seek higher income and access to better schooling.
15. (8)_____
16. (1)_People of color move from segregated southern states.

For clarification, the thirteenth line is a repeat of the seventh line, the fourteenth line is a repeat of the third line; the fifteenth line is a repeat of the eighth line, the sixteenth line is a repeat of the first line in the poem. Teachers will be able to assess what learners know about the unit from what learners are communicating as facts of the Northern Migration when the students propose lines that extend, expand, and reinforce information offered in previous lines. Teachers should encourage learners to listen attentively to each other, raise questions, address contradictions, and even correct facts voiced by peers as the pantoum poem is generated.

Your pantoum may look something like this:

Northern Migration for Different Reasons

People of color moved north from segregated southern states.
African Americans migrate from the rural south to the urban north.
Several groups seek higher income and access to better schooling.
Mexican Americans move north, often for better farm jobs

African Americans migrate from rural south to urban north.
Many Blacks move from Alabama, Mississippi and Louisiana.
Mexican Americans move north, often for better farm jobs.
Many Latinx leave their homes in New Mexico and move to California.
Many Blacks move from Alabama, Mississippi and Louisiana.
Factory jobs in Michigan, Illinois, and Pennsylvania attract new migrants.
Many New Mexicans leave homes in New Mexico and move to California.
Years as migrant workers, moving from farm to farm await these Mexicanx.
Mexican Americans move north, often for better farm jobs.
Several groups seek higher income and access to better schooling.
Many New Mexicans leave homes in New Mexico and move to California.
People of color move north from segregated southern states.

Choose a Person, Place or Event from Your Studies and Write a Pantoum Poem

1. *Begin by writing four original lines.*

1	
2	
3	
4	

2. *REPEAT lines 2 and 4 and expand ideas in lines 5 and 6:*

2	
5	
4	
6	

3. *REPEAT lines 5 and 6, expand ideas in lines 7 and 8:*

5	
7	
6	
8	

4. *FINALLY, repeat lines 1, 3, 7 and 8 in the following order:*

7	
3	
8	
1	

5. *Write your title at the top of your final draft and at the bottom the COUNTRY, NAME of person, place or event that is the subject of your poem*

Adapted by Anna J. Small Roseboro teachingenglishlanguagearts.com

FIGURE 2.2 Worksheet for Drafting a Pantoum Poem Adapted by Author.

Poem: Acrostic

Another option is inviting students to write an acrostic poem about a person, place, or event based on a student-selected picture. The sample poem I have written and shared here, "She Persisted (Ella Persistió)," is about one of the women active in the labor rights movement in Southern California in the 1960s. You will note that an acrostic poem uses the letters in the name of the person, place, or event as the first letter in words about that person, place, or event.

Dolores Huerta, a person born in 1930 during the target historical period, only became an active leader later in her life. The students will see, however, that her story aligns with the broader concept of Northern Migration because her ancestors migrated north from New Mexico to Stockton, California. Senora Huerta became co-founder with Cesar Chavez of the United Farm Workers Union. The photo a student selects will determine whether the acrostic poem they write centers on a person, place, or even an event.

To help the students decide on the person, ask them to consider these Five Ws and H questions about their person in the way they can be asked about Dolores Huerta:

- Who is Señora Huerta?
- What events spurred her leadership?
- When was she an active labor organizer?
- When was she the most active labor leader?
- Where did she migrate to?
- Why did she migrate to Stockton?
- How did she mobilize workers?

In contrast to pantoum poem writing, acrostic poetry production has students write the letters of their chosen person, place, or event down the left side of a blank paper, tablet, or laptop. Then, using concrete nouns, active verbs, and evocative adjectives that begin with each letter, they write a poem that answers as many of the who, what, when, where, why, and how questions as possible within the time allotted for this in-class activity (Figure 2.3).

FIGURE 2.3 Public Domain Photo of Dolores Huerta, Activist with United Farm Workers Union.

She Persisted (Ella Persistió)
D...devoted and determined
O...observant and optimistic
L... labor-minded lady
O...organizing orator
R...respected and reliable
E...effervescent and emphatic
S...smart, sold-out sister

H...heartfelt helper
U...undaunted and understanding
E...endeavored exuberantly
R...revered and reliable
T...tough and triumphant
A...acknowledged at last

Poem: Elegy

A third option of poetry writing for history learning is to have students choose a key person about whom they have learned from class texts or during homework searches of recommended websites. Subsequently, based on learner knowledge about the historical figure from a quick online search, write an elegy or a short poem highlighting valuable contributions of this person that speak to DIJE (diversity, inclusion, justice, or equity) teaching related to the target historical period. An elegy is a poem that laments the passing of an admirable person, articulating what that person has done that is praiseworthy.

Next is a commemorative poem about Arturo Alfonso Schomburg, a major archiver of literature and art reflecting this historical period of the Harlem Renaissance.

Arturo Alfonso Schomburg (January 24, 1874 – June 10, 1938) was a historian, writer, collector, and activist on the Eastern coast of the United States during the period between the two World Wars. His academic work is esteemed so much that he has been recognized for naming a famous library in Harlem, the Schomburg Library, for scholars across the globe to conduct cutting-edge research. If your students are like I was, they may assume that Schomburg likely was a wealthy Jewish man who supported the work of African Americans living in Harlem during that historical period. You will note, however, that he is a Puerto Rican of African and German descent who acknowledged his multicultural heritage as a multi-racial immigrant (Figure 2.4).

FIGURE 2.4 Public Domain photo of Arturo Alfonso Schomburg, Activist, Historian and Bilbiophile.

Elegy poem writing for historical learning works best when teachers invite learners to draw from the learner's own culture and ancestry. Direct students to locate someone who lived during the historical period of the unit just completed whose ethnic background is the same as that of students in class. This pedagogical approach personalizes the elegy poem writing and history learning experience. Depending on the details in the class textbook, students may need to read a short overview online of this historical person to be able to write a poem that summarizes what they have learned and that reveals what the student now knows. Consider the sentence starters: WHO, WHAT, WHEN, WHERE, WHY, and HOW again. You will see that Figure 2.5 is a photo of the front of the Schomburg Library in Harlem, and this Center for Research could be used for the place poem.

FIGURE 2.5 Photograph of Schomburg Center for Research in Black Culture.

The following is an example of an elegy poem of Arturo Schomburg written by Anna J. Small Roseboro in response to an online writing prompt of the OPENWRITE virtual group of educators who meet monthly to share writing prompts to consider in their in-classroom teaching.

Now They Know Better

They told him his folks had no history.
He spent years proving them wrong.
He collected books and arts and letters
Proving contributions to culture and song

He immigrated to the USA and joined the band,
not as a musician but as an archiving man.
During the years of the Harlem Renaissance
This Afro-Puerto Rican man took a stand

Schomburg joined intellectuals there
They had done so much and had so much to say
about their participation in progress of this nation.
inventors and educators skilled in business and science
records collected and preserved for all who would question

Because of his passion and knowledge
He was successful working at Fisk college
He used what he learned, misinformation he spurned
When the library he built these rumors he kil't.
and now you can visit yourself.
Check the art on the wall and the books on the shelf.

Employing poetry as a writing-to-learn strategy involves offering learners various options in the poetry writing process. "Content teachers can successfully introduce various types of poetry that describe and illuminate factual information on topics specific to content classes." And, further, "Writing demands active involvement in the learning process. It encourages students to remember..., discover..., and to think through ideas..." (McWhorter & Bullion-Mears, 2015, p. 46). As in the activities above, pantoum, acrostic, and elegy poem production in a history class gives learners multiple opportunities to absorb and display content material on the Northern Migration on the East or West sides of the United States.

Grading Poetry for Content, Not Form

Many educators ask how to grade poetry written to assess student knowledge of subject matter such as history, social studies, or geography rather than how well students write a particular kind or style of poem for an English class. Responses to this question are rooted in other questions.

- Does the poem reveal accurate facts about the assigned topic?
- Is there a minimum number of distracting errors in learner writing that cloud the communication of the poem's message?
- Is there something extra creative in the poem that bolsters the reading experience to the point where anyone who reads it would say, "WOW! This is a great poem?"

In other words, use a general grading guideline like the one shown in Figure 2.6. This graphic depicts grade C as the sea because the content is complete; B is the boat sailing on the sea because the content is complete and correct, and A is the sail fluttering above the boat that reflects a complete, correct, and creative poem, paper, product or presentation. D means the work needs to be improved and include the required components of the assignment, and F means the student failed to submit the evidence work called for in the assignment.

Recall that the writing of a poem in the history, geography, and social studies content area classroom is primarily a formative assessment. In other words, the goal is for the teacher to measure student learning. Accordingly, consider an "alternative" evaluation of student poetry writing by collecting, reading, and marking the poems in a grade book with

- A check for complete (poem includes facts that reveal the student understands who, what, when, where, why, and how of the period).
- Check-minus for incomplete; a key component is missing.
- A minus for "failed to turn in a poem."

♦ A check plus is needed to show how a poem contains enhanced poetic features beyond those required in the basic content.

GENERAL GRADING GUIDELINES

- A = Complete, Correct, and Creative
- B = Complete and Correct
- C = Complete
- D = Deficient
- F = Failing, for now

C = THE **SEA** –**Complete** (includes all components of the assignment)

B = THE **BOAT** – Complete and **Correct** (rides on the sea with minimal errors in mechanics, usage, grammar, and spelling

A = THE **SAIL** – Complete, Correct and **Creative** (something above and beyond the boat, original and fresh elements enhancing the final presentation, performance/product

FIGURE 2.6 General Grading Guidelines, created by the author using art from MS Office 365.

In-Class Student Feedback

When students return from the long holiday break, plan an in-class activity in which the students read and rate the poems of others in the class. For example, randomly or purposefully select five to seven poems to put into each folder, along with a copy of a rubric based on the assignment sheet. This sheet should remind students that the assignment was to write a poem in one of three formats: an acrostic, an elegy, or a pantoum, using accurate facts about the WHO, WHAT, WHEN, WHERE, WHY, and HOW of the target historical period. Learners will read and respond to poems in folders assigned to their groups.

Consider various ways to assign poems to learners for peer review. One pathway is dividing the class into groups that equal the number of folders and assigning each group a color or letter to correspond with that color or letter of the folder. Groups may review and give feedback on a poem that includes poems from someone in their group. It's okay if one of the folders has the reader's poem. In such an instance, the poem's author can interrogate his or her own poetry writing and knowledge of this topic of study.

Random Grouping for In-Class Work

Consider using an online random group generator like that found on the website *Random Lists*. I like to have a chart prepared to share or show that says something as simple as:

- A-Blue reads B-Green and C-Red
- B-Green reads C-Red and D-Orange
- C-Red reads D-Orange and E- Purple
- D- Orange reads E-Purple and A-Red
- E-Purple reads A-Red and B-Green

In other words, students seated as groups receive the first color-coded folder and just read the poems, one at a time, passing the poem to the right when the buzzer rings. Set the buzzer to ring every 45-60 seconds for the reading. Adjust time as needed for the students you're teaching. Then, have students complete the rubric for the poem last read. Set the timer for two minutes or so for the reading, reflection, and rating. Then, collect the folders and pass them to the next group. Repeat the process of reading, passing to the right, and reading and rating the last poem read. Following this sequence, students will have experienced eight to ten poems in about 15 to 20 minutes. You collect the folders, review the rubrics, and return them to the poets the next day.

Benefits of In-Class Reading and Rating

Reading peers' poems in this setting serves as another "review" of what students have been learning. Teachers may schedule the final 15 minutes of class for students to meet in triads to select a poem written by a peer that best reflects the criteria of the poem writing assignment about the designated content topic. Depending on the number of students in class that day, ask them to locate a pantoum, acrostic, or an elegy in the folder to read aloud to the class. One spokesperson from the triad or group can then stand and read their classmate's poem aloud.

If it is convenient, project the poem on the classroom screen for the class to see as students listen to a read-aloud of a peer's poem. Whole-group reading of a learner's poem while listening to it can further reinforce content facts that a teacher intends for learners to retain. This visual and auditory experience will further enhance the students who are more visual or auditory learners. Furthermore, reading original poetry aloud can foster trust and empathy in the classroom community.

Writing by Hand Reinforces Learning

To acquire current evidence of the value of assignments I'd used for years, I contacted a teacher of English language arts at a local middle school with whom I had worked in the past. She consented, again, to collaborate. We decided to do the field test in her class of sixth graders who study Michigan history in their social studies classes.

This teacher and I decided to do the pre-writing by posting general questions on slides, then having pairs complete an acrostic of the letters in Michigan State, using nouns, verbs, and modifiers that fit what the students know and are learning in their Social Studies classes. We planned to create a word bank as the teacher wrote the words the students thought of and verbalized when called upon. But things happened, and we didn't have a written word bank for students to view. But they remembered quite a few.

The teacher brought in picture books from the library, a couple of globes, and some Petoskey stones which are colorful stones unique to Michigan lakesides. After directing them to view the picture or artifact, we invited them to write a personal pantoum poem. The goal was to glean from the viewing, discussions, and sharing of their acrostic poems.

We began drafting a pantoum poem using prompts on the slides and the ideas they recalled from creating their acrostics. The students described their own memories and experiences in and about the state of Michigan. What a joy to see students admit for the first time, according to the teacher, that they descended from one of the tribes of Native Americans who lived in this area or were of French descent, one of the colonizers. The students were making personal connections in this humanizing activity. The topic did not seem so distant to their classmates.

I provided a handout similar to Figure 2.2. The students wrote along, following prompts projected from my PowerPoint presentation. Once completed, we planned to have them read aloud their poems to their elbow partners very quietly so they could hear what they wrote without disturbing their classmates. Reading aloud is an efficient way to see what is working and what needs revision.

The teacher planned to have the students share these pantoums in the next class meeting. But since we didn't finish during the time I was there, she decided to use my slide deck and start the assignment all over. Since she taught English Language Arts, she had an opportunity to see how the students responded to the jargon of writing, and they crafted poems about their study in Social Studies.

This combination of generating words and phrases together as they viewed pictures and manipulated artifacts and writing a structured poem that need not have a rhyme or rhythm pattern provided an efficient assessment of what the students were learning in Social Studies. The ELA teacher could also monitor how her young teenagers used words and phrases to express themselves, collaborate with peers, and present their writing to the class.

Working with these energetic 6th graders in a conference room at their school library, I noticed as I walked around that these 6th graders had difficulty manipulating pencils. Between time away from school during COVID-19 and the fact that they do most of their work on laptops and Chrome books, few have developed strong handwriting muscles.

I wonder if the hands-on, heuristic advantages that come with thinking about what to say and figuring out how to express it in script will be lost for this age group. Because so much research about writing to learn shows that students who physically write and draw retain a majority of what they learn, teachers must support students in writing about what they are learning in students' own words for greater learning retention. Educators McGill and Miller from a high school in southern California, shared with me similar effects of handwriting when I was conducting research on this topic way back in 1989.

Research compels teachers in all content areas to consider ways to incorporate a range of writing opportunities in their lessons. As you mull over whether this practice is worthwhile, please know that handwriting, in and of itself, is a heuristic, a way of knowing. As students search for words to express themselves, they think about what they know and what they are able to do. To be beneficial, the teacher does not have to collect, read, or grade writing assigned for this purpose. It can be used to prepare for talking about newly taught concepts and reflecting on ones being practiced. Occasionally, for quizzes and tests, teachers may substitute questions requiring students to explain how to solve problems, why a certain chemical reaction occurred, or historical event impacts social justice. In this case, the writing is graded for clarity and accuracy.

A February 2024 *Scientific American* article in "Hands On" by Charlotte Hu confirms this theory:

> A recent study in Frontiers in Psychology monitored brain activity in students taking notes and found that those writing by hand had higher levels of electrical activity across a wide range of interconnected brain regions responsible for movement, vision, sensory processing, and memory. The findings add to a growing body of evidence that has many experts speaking up about the

importance of teaching children to handwrite words and draw pictures.

Reflecting on this in-class experience further reinforces my advocacy for this formative assessment activity. Since reading what students write can help you diagnose specific deficiencies more quickly and measure their understanding of the various content-specific concepts and their application, inviting students to do assignments described here can stimulate metacognition and verbalization. Allotting class time for creating and handwriting poems in short, focused forms can be a valuable addition to teaching tools because it has multiple benefits for student learning and retention.

Closing Thoughts: Valuable Reinforcement of Teaching with Visuals

Note the vibrant value of poetry writing for true content learning. This value appears when

- for homework or in class, students will have
  - viewed several websites with photos reflecting the historical period just studied.
  - chosen a person, place, or event from graphics on one or more selected websites.
- in class, before the break, the students will have:
  - written a group poem in class under teacher guidance.
  - drafted a poem of their own in their choice of genre
    - that demonstrated their incorporation into a genre of writing.
    - writing in a form that requires a careful selection of words and facts to meet the class assignment.
- in class, after the long break, students will have
  - read and rated two poems written by their peers.
  - chosen a sample poem in the assigned style and topic for their group.
- seen and heard poems by their peers read aloud.

Another takeaway from poetry peer-review writing for content learning is that teachers learn about what their students know or do not know about a content unit. Such teacher knowledge aids in adapting or devising lessons to fill in gaps in learner knowledge or understanding before the major unit exam. Secondary history and social studies teachers aim to induce ways of knowing so learners begin to think like historians, scientists, geographers, and so on (Moje, 2015). By default, poetry writing can build disciplinary thinking in creative and engaging ways that foster humanizing learning communities, inspire inclusivity, and reflect respect for those we aspire to teach, with and from whom we learn.

The learning value for students starts with the pedagogical choices the teachers make but centers on and ends with the intellectual prowess of learners. Teachers create the spaces for student learning, but students do the actual learning. The students do the work, not their teachers. Teachers are offering students choices within the teacher's control of options. Teachers who care genuinely about student learning honor students' writing by cultivating a classroom where students take on the authority of their learning through a combination of tasks such as reading and rating the poems of their peers, followed by hearing three to five poems of their peers read aloud.

As I close this description of a tried-and-true classroom teaching strategy, I must acknowledge the assistance of an experienced colleague, Nalova Westbrook, who helped me prepare this chapter and affirm my experience by sharing academic research that supports the ideas of incorporating poetry writing in courses across the curriculum. I, too, continue to learn as I collaborate with colleagues across the content areas. And just because this book is about the value of poetry writing, I'll tie things up with a poem. I must confess. I hope the answer to the closing questions is not "Yes."

What? Think?

Student talk teaches
Them to talk and to listen
Reading widely teaches
Them to read and to reflect
Writing regularly teaches them to write
To express themselves
And to expound their thoughts
Why do we teachers try to curb any
When all three teach students to think?
Is thinking the problem?
A problem we're seeking to quench?

References

Bean, T. W., Readence, J. E., & Baldwin, R. S. (2011). *Content area literacy: An integrated approach.* Kendall Hunt.

Bean, T. W., Readence, J. E., & Dunkerly-Bean, J. (2017). *Content area literacy: An integrated approach* (11th ed.). Kendall Hunt.

Chaucer, G. (2008). *The Canterbury tales.* (Original work published ca. 1400). Modern Library.

Ellison, R. (1952). *Invisible man.* Random House.

Fisher, D., & Frey, N. (2021). *Better learning through structured teaching: A framework for gradually releasing responsibility* (3rd ed.). ASCD.

Gorrell, N., & Colfax, E. (2012). *Writing poetry through the eyes of science: A teacher's guide to scientific literacy and poetic response* (p. 202). Equinox.

Houghton Mifflin Company. (1996). *The American heritage college dictionary* (3rd ed.). Houghton Mifflin.

Hu, C. (2024, February 21). *Hands-on. Scientific American.* Springer Nature America. www.scientificamerican.com

Januchowski-Hartley, S. R., Sopinka, N., Merkle, B. G., Lux, C., Zivian, A., Goff, P., & Oester, S. (2018). Poetry as a creative practice to enhance engagement and learning in conservation science. *BioScience, 68*(11), 905–911. https://doi.org/10.1093/biosci/biy105

Lee, L. (1983). *Colored people's time* (Illustrated ed.). S. French.

Library of Congress. (n.d.). *Photos, prints, drawings*. Retrieved September 25, 2024, from www.loc.gov/photos/collections/

McWhorter, J. Y., & Bullion-Mears, A. (2015). *Understanding literacy through literature and content areas*. Pearson Education.

Moje, E. B. (2015). Doing and teaching disciplinary literacy with adolescent learners: A social and cultural enterprise. *Harvard Educational Review, 85*(2), 254–278. https://doi.org/10.17763/0017-8055.85.2.254

Roseboro, A. J. S. (n.d.). *Organizing a week of speeches*. Teaching to Inspire. Retrieved September 25, 2024, from https://teachingenglishlanguagearts.com/organizing-a-week-of-speeches/

Shange, N. (1976). *For colored girls who have considered suicide / when the rainbow is enuf*. Macmillan.

VARK Learn Limited. (n.d.). *Teaching and learning styles*. Retrieved September 25, 2024, from https://vark-learn.com/product/teaching-and-learning-styles/

3

Poetic Pathways to Comprehension

Sarah J. Donovan

In mid-February, our 8th-grade team launched our annual unit on the Holocaust. History and English language arts (ELA) partnered on the content. At the same time, Science and Math did some decidedly more light-hearted content to give learners a break from the intensity of atrocities. As the ELA teacher, I framed our work around how artists (e.g., writers, illustrators, screenwriters) represent what is unimaginable including the decisions they make to care for the reader/viewer when showing scenes of atrocities. I thought I had a great activity: to tap into prior experiences by reading a picture book *Terrible Things* (Bunting), which is an allegory.

Briefly, there is a forest full of animals, and one, abstract terrible thing takes away a flock, a herd, a colony. Each time, the other groups are relieved it is not them and do nothing to stop the terrible thing until what remains is a single white rabbit. Because I planned this unit with a variety of texts—the memoir *Night* by Elie Wiesel and the film *Life is Beautiful* (Benigni, 1997)—I knew the goal of the unit was to compare the choices the creators made to tell the story of the Holocaust. I felt good about that, but where I struggled (and still do sometimes) is what students do *after*

DOI: 10.4324/9781003587262-3

instruction or an activity to show their learning (what I intended for them to learn and what additional discoveries I may not have anticipated). In other words, after what I think is a great lesson, I found myself saying *so what do you think* or take this quiz. Inevitably, my assessments were too broad or too narrow to offer time and space for students to synthesize the learning and show their meaning-making process.

After the powerful conclusion of *Terrible Things* (a single survivor tasked with sharing what they witnessed), students had this expression on their faces that told me they were processing what they read; they instinctively turned to their elbow partner to chat about the story. I heard some say it reminded them of the Holocaust. I heard some wonder why the bunny who lived was white and what white might symbolize. Some were quiet, and I had no idea what they were thinking, but I hoped they were processing the story rather than thinking about lunch (or both). I had prepared, you guessed it, a quiz for them to answer on a worksheet, which felt like I was undoing this shared experience. The assessment was narrow as aligned with the concrete "measurable goals" in my objective, and it also undermined my students' capacity to show what they were coming to understand.

Authors rarely want readers to answer multiple-choice questions after reading a story. To extend this logic to other content areas, historians may want students to know the facts, but they want students to know how the facts were gleaned from primary documents, who created such documents, why, and for whom. Language teachers want students to know words, but they also want students to use those words to communicate, to create.

Cognitive psychologist Edmund Huey (1908) asserted that the goal of reading is to create meaning and along with Piaget's (1952) work of schema theory and Vygotsky's (1978) scaffolding—we know that prior knowledge and experiences affect new knowledge. Louise Rosenblatt's seminal text *Literature as Exploration* (1938) affirmed the critical role of the learner in the creation of meaning (i.e., meaning from the written text, your lecture, a video, social media, a song). Meaning is not in the text for the teacher to cover or for the author to transmit. Meaning is created in the interaction between the learner and the text (written, verbal, visual, gestural). Whether the text is a picture book, novel, film, or slide deck-based lecture, teachers need to be interested in the interaction between the learner and the text; this is the space where students can bring their past learning and experiences to new ideas before and around them. This interaction extends and expands student learning.

Learners need time and space to make meaning, and one way to support students in this process is to encourage them to engage in the poetic process. This is not about the product but the process of drawing on the *text* and their own lived experiences/knowledge to create something new and thus learn.

Improving Literacy and Academic Outcomes

One recommended avenue for improving the literacy and academic outcomes of middle-grade and secondary students is to provide literacy instruction across the content areas (e.g., Carnegie Council on Advancing Adolescent Literacy, 2010; Heller & Greenleaf, 2007; Kamil et al., 2008). Literacy instruction means making that interactional space between the reader and the text visible. As teacher educators, we know that content area teachers may struggle to incorporate reading and writing instruction into their classes; maybe this is because listening and reading seem to be basic tasks not specific to concepts in their subject area (Wineburg, 2001). Another reason is that few teacher preparation programs offer specific reading and writing pedagogy courses for all content areas.

Writing poetry is one practice to enhance content-focused reading comprehension skills in secondary students (Hanauer, 2010; Vaughn, Swanson et al., 2015). Writing poetry as a form of comprehension is a writing-based reading comprehension intervention that integrates effective literacy practices within all content instruction. Teachers use instructional practices to engage students in the content through vocabulary, text reading, and discussion to improve student understanding of the content. Writing poetry makes this process visible. Further, writing poetry aligns with current standards in content area literacy, reading, and writing (e.g., Common Core State Standards), which emphasize higher-level reasoning and thinking about text and content rather than simple acquisition of factual information. The *Terrible Things* example described above exemplifies how a multiple choice worksheet to check for comprehension is lower-level reasoning and thinking about the text that invites guessing or process-of-elimination work rather than synthesizing ideas or puzzling through connections, implications, and relationships of ideas.

Instructionally, the poetry writing model I show below in three lessons emphasizes writing about text so students can elaborate on important content, better integrate new ideas into their working understanding of the content, and more accurately revisit elements of the newly learned content at subsequent points in time (Applebee et al., 2003; Beck & McKeown, 2006; Eva-Wood, 2009).

The instructional practices in poetry writing with content areas come from research on poetry literacy and literacy learning practices associated with improved outcomes for individuals with learning difficulties (Cook & Bennett, 2022; Hanauer, 2012; Langer, 1979). These practices included (a) purposeful content learning goals, (b) a method for gathering content language and ideas such as a notebook or graphic organizer; (c) instruction in vocabulary and concept development related to building background knowledge, (d) supported opportunities to synthesize the content in a poetic form, and (e) self-assessment to reflect on the learning process. The role of the teacher is to model their thinking and synthesis processes and offer feedback (including praise) while students write. Writing poetry, rather than a quiz, is a way to support a degree of individual accountability but more for the sake of learning than compliance (Gajria et al., 2007; Gersten et al., 2006; Swanson et al., 2012).

Our argument here and in this book is that poetry is a teaching tool for content learning and a medium for exploring their learning experience (Ofsted, 2007).

A Focus on Comprehension

We know that learning is a combination of cognitive and affective processes. The poetic process shows the transaction of the text and learning in a new text form. While the new text will be an artifact of learning, the process of meaning-making is more important.

When students write relational poetry—poetry derived from a text—they draw on so many cognitive processes:

- *Summary*: They show they understand who, what, where, when, how, and why.
- *Synthesis*: They synthesize what they knew and now know; they may draw on their personal lived experiences (family, hobbies) and/or prior learning, texts (including films, Netflix, TikTok, and other classes).
- *Analysis*: They draw on keywords/jargon from the text (again, this could be your lecture, the video, the textbook, or an article) to shape their poem; they name the rhetorical moves of facts, evidence, and claims; they name the language as absolute, concrete, abstract
- *Comparison*: They can show multiple voices, relationships between ideas, and various perspectives.
- *Critical and creative thinking*: They interpret and make claims in their poems about what the text means and its implications.

What Does a Poetic Pathway Look Like in the Classroom?

To foster a dynamic and engaging poetry writing experience, it is essential to guide students through a structured approach that emphasizes inspiration, process, and reflection. First, I will offer you an overview of the process, and then I will show you three examples of using poetry to demonstrate comprehension: 1) "Something You Should Know," writing poetry to explore thought leaders in a content area; 2) "Where I'm From," writing poetry to compare concepts; and 3) "X Tells Me to Be," writing poetry to interpret the significance of concepts.

An Overview of the Poetry Writing Process

Begin by providing students with *inspiration* that aligns with their learning goals, whether through a specific poetic prompt, a mentor text, or a thematic concept. A mentor text is an example of the poem form to use as a resource, inspiration, and graphic organizer. Next, introduce the *process* by demonstrating how to personally connect to the prompt and imitate the *mentor text*. A mentor text can be a poem that shows the concept and structure you want students to work on within the lesson. You may project the mentor text on a screen. However, we recommend that you make printouts to tape into students' notebooks or offer students access to a virtual file to copy and paste into their digital notebooks. Now, do a think-aloud about the mentor text, observe and discuss its features, and then show your writing process. Then it is *your turn* (the students' turn to write). Invite students to work on their poems while you actively engage in the same process to model the journey of drafting a poem. Allot five to seven minutes depending on your students' writing stamina.

Encourage students to pair-share their work and discuss their creative processes, highlighting how they incorporated the inspiration concept and personal experiences into their writing. In the sharing, the students and you show the various experiences that come when a writer interacts with texts (e.g., the prompt, the teachers' thinking, the mentor text).

This process will repeat after a conceptual lesson, and students will write a second poem that includes new learning. This comprehensive approach not only deepens students' understanding of writing poetry but also enhances their critical thinking and language development skills with new content.

Here is an overview:

1. *Inspiration*: Give, read, or offer the students the inspiration for poetic thinking.

2. *Process*:
   a. Show students the mentor text;
   b. Paste this into their notebook on the left page;
   c. Invite students to tell you what they notice; point out what students might notice such as the way the poem starts, the number of lines, the punctuation, and the ending;
   d. Model your thinking or approach to the writing process;
   e. Show how you use the notes from your content lesson to help you write.
3. *Your turn*:
   a. Set a timer for students to write five to seven minutes. You do it, too. They should see you going from the text to the writing, scratching out words, rearranging. It can be messy.
   b. Invite students to pair-share the poem. Students should read aloud rather than give their poems to a peer to read so that they can hear how the language and line breaks create rhythm and ideas. Offer students sentence stems (see below) to respond to one another.
4. *Introduce new vocabulary and concepts*. See the three sample lessons below.
5. *Conceptual poem*: Now invite students to write a poem that synthesizes the content into a new poem.
6. *Pair-Share*: Facilitate peer and self-assessment or metacognition: Ask students to talk through what information they drew on from the lesson to help them write the poem, what ideas came from their experiences, where their unique voice (joke, clever twist) comes into play in show meaning-making, and what they are learning from their peer's poem and process.
7. *Publication*: Students will share their poems in various ways to have an authentic audience, share their learning, and nurture community together.
8. *Grading/Evaluation*: You will use a conceptual-based rubric to evaluate comprehension and assign a grade if needed.

9. *Reflection/Adaptation*: As a teacher, what did you learn about the content from your students' texts and the poem–circuit created between you and them through your experience of their poetry? What did you learn about your students? What will you do next, tomorrow?

Let us see how this sequence works in a few lessons to adapt to any content area.

Sample Lesson: Something You Should Know About Influencers

In this lesson, I walk you through how I would use the poem prompt "Something You Should Know" to get to know various thought leaders in a specific content area. I take you right into the lesson, zooming into what I would say and then zooming out for some of my meta-moments about why and how.

Students write "Something You Should Know" poems to show what they learned about historical figures. In crafting a poem about how historical, social, and cultural issues or events impacted a thought leader, students synthesize a great deal of information in a concentrated form to capture the essence of that figure.

Consider the Spanish language standard for reading and literature. One standard, in particular, asks students to *investigate and report on ways in which a writer has influenced or been influenced by historical, social, and cultural issues or events*. We hope you can immediately see how all content areas can follow this plan by replacing "writers" with influential economists, scientists, geologists, mathematicians, artists, musicians, and so on.

Inspiration

To begin, introduce the day's writing prompt: "Something You Should Know." Ask students to open up their paper or digital notebook and follow along as you do the same in your notebook projected onto the whiteboard or by writing directly only on the whiteboard.

| Sarah: | *Today, we are thinking about how places and experiences in those places shape who we are and become.* |

Process

| Sarah: | *In your notebook, make a list of the places you have lived, spent time, experienced significant events, and even worked (for students who have had jobs). (Table 3.1 shows my list as it might look on the whiteboard, as well as how your students might put it in their notebook.)* |

TABLE 3.1 Poem Idea Gathering Chart

Places I lived	*Places I spent time*	*Significant events*	*Worked*
• Small house in a suburb of Chicago with 10 siblings • Double-wide trailer in a Fort Myers retirement community (even though I was not retired) • A house with cows in the backyard (not mine) in Oklahoma	• Gyms lifting weights • Beaches playing volleyball • Favorite park swinging and jumping onto wood chips • Walking the highway 3 miles a day	• I played varsity volleyball as a freshman (did not go well) • My parents divorced • I never won anything…	• Burger King • Limited • Pharmacy • Pizza place • Prison • Schools

| Sarah (continued): | *Now, choose one that stands out to you that you think that, if people knew this about you, they would understand who you are now better. Choose something you feel comfortable* |

sharing with a classmate. I would choose to work at the pizza place. I do not mind sharing that, and it has influenced who I am today. However, how do I write about this?

At this point, students will need a mentor text. We recommend printing copies of this poem and having students paste it in their notebooks to imitate the form if needed. Poet Clint Smith wrote a fantastic mentor text poem called "Something You Should Know." This poem is a great alternative to slideshows and essays for reporting the ways individuals have been influenced by people, places, and events in broad and specific ways. Here is an example from teacher Gayle Sands and her legacy as National Spelling Bee Champion.

Something You Should Know by Gayle Sands

Something you should know about me
is that I was
the National Spelling Bee Champion
of Chautauqua County, New York
for four years running, and made it
to the state competition
at the New York State Fair.

I didn't win.
That, unfortunately,
was as close as I came
to being a winner.
As a claim to fame,
it was pretty pathetic.

I studied the dictionary,
carried around
the little booklet
of Really Hard Words
and surreptitiously boned up

on esoteric spellings
when I finished early in class.
I was a word wizard.
A phonics phenom.
A spelling savant.

When I was in the Spelling Zone,
words wrote themselves
in the space above my head.
All I had to do was read them aloud.

I wanted to be Julie Malinoski,
who was a cheerleader
and a gymnast
and was small and blonde
and whose nose turned up just so.
Instead, I was the
Buffalo Evening News
Spelling Bee champion
of Chautauqua County.

You probably didn't know that about me.

Sarah: *Notice how Gayle begins "Something you should know about me/is that I was" and then goes on to share an important event, what happened, and how it impacted her. She did go on to become an English teacher.*

Your Turn

Sarah: *Now that I have a mentor text to help me get started. I am ready to write. "Something you should know about me/is that I was a waitress at Aurelio's Pizza when I was 14…" Now tell your elbow partner what you will write about. Okay, let us take 5 minutes and see what we can do. I am going to write, too. As* *we write, remember our norm of no-walk/no-talk to respect this writing time.*

As the teacher, you should write a few lines of your poem and then move around the room to check in on students. If they are stuck, help them talk through the first two lines and invite them to talk through their event or experience. Then, turn them back to the writing. I carry my notebook as I move around the room, drafting my poem. I scan the room to see if anyone needs support.

Pair-Share

After five minutes or so, invite students to do a pair share. They can just read what they have to a neighbor. Maybe offer a kind response from the rhetorical triangle:

- Logos: I learned a new fact, which is... Thank you.
- Pathos: When you said X, I felt Y.
- Ethos: You seem to have expertise in... or your writing is great because it was vivid, sensory, and rhythmic.

Again, it is best if you model this first. Read your poem and invite a few students to say something nice to you using the sentence stems.

Sarah: *(You probably want to hear my poem?) Okay, so I have a first draft of my poem. I am going to read it to you. Can I have 2 people respond to show how this might look and feel?*

Something you should know
is that as a 14-year-old, I once worked at a pizza place.
I prepped the antipasto salad
washing dozens of romaine heads,
slicing ham Julien style.

I filled cannoli shells
with chocolate chip ricotta mix
and rolled the ends in pistachios.
And some days I was the only
waitress, slinging pizzas for
20 tables, calculating tabs in
my head while bussing tables. Perhaps
that is why, even now, I dream of
forgotten drink orders or disappointing
customers, and I am so afraid
of letting someone down.

Student 1: *I learned that being a waitress involved much consideration. That may be why you are so organized now—like when you said, "20 tables!"*

Student 2: *When you said, "I dream of forgotten drink orders." I can relate. Sometimes I dream of forgetting to do my homework.*

Sarah: *Thanks. So now, you will do that for each other. Remember to receive your compliment with a "thanks."*

Now for Your Content: Influencers

At this point, students are thinking about how our lived experiences shape who we are and may become. The above sequence may be enough for the day, but you may find that you have more time, so you can move into introducing the concept.

Now you might say that the day's lesson is something we should know about an important thinker in our content area.

To use Spanish class as our example, we will look at contemporary authors from Spanish-speaking countries and communities who have been influential in literature. Students can create a list of influencers/thought leaders, or you can create one. I used these two sources: Latinx in Kid Lit, specifically the Pura Belpré Award Winners, and REFORMA, the National Association to Promote Library & Information Services to Latinos and the Spanish Speaking.

- Pura Teresa Belpré y Nogueras, Afro-Puerto Rican
- Marisol Ceh Moo, Mexican Maya
- Humberto Ak'pabal, K'iche Maya Guatemala
- Pablo Neruda, Chilean
- Federico Garcia Lorca, Spanish
- Jorge Luis Borges, Argentine
- Julia Alvarez, Dominican
- Gabriel Garcia Márquez, Columbian
- Laura Esquivel, Mexican
- Sandra Cisneros, Chicano
- Elizabeth Acevedo, Dominican-American
- Margarita Engle, Cuban-American
- Yuyi Morales, Mexican
- Javier Zamora, Mexican

When designing a lesson around a standard, we unpack its keywords. For example, what does it mean to be *an influencer* of or *to be influenced by historical, social, and cultural issues or events*?

If we think about *historical* events, that seems fairly clear: past events. So, in looking at a person's life, we want to consider what was going on in their country when they were growing up or making their mark in a particular field. The event could be national, within their country, or international, a conflict between countries. *Social* issues are sometimes considered social problems.

The question is "problem for who" or who or what perceives it as a problem. A social issue may mean a condition that negatively affects the personal or social lives of individuals. This can imply social justice. Framing social issues along the lines of the well-being of individuals, communities, or larger groups helps us see the relationships between historical events, policies, and social systems (e.g., the economy, government, and policies) on human beings. Some social problems are also caused by or exacerbated by historical events. However, sometimes, it is related to geological events like a hurricane or the community's geographic location, which may have a history of conflict, colonization, and/or limited or special access to resources.

Suppose a cultural group lives on land with incredible resources. In that case, they may be exploited by another country or social group to gain access to those resources (e.g., water, fertile soil, and oil). Some social conditions that can impact individuals or social groups include the following: poverty, health care, education, economic inequality, climate change, immigration, unemployment, politics, violence, religion, disease, ageism, crime, homelessness, obesity, substance abuse, racial discrimination, gender inequality, and homophobia.

Now consider cultural issues or events. Culture uncovers a broad range of experiences specifically related to a cultural group. Cultural events that influence an individual or cause an individual to lead or advocate for change may be caused by historical or geographical events and exacerbated by social problems for a particular group within a country, specifically related to the cultural group's or subgroup's perceived identities (e.g., race, ethnicity, language, religion, sexual orientation, gender, and disability).

Culture also is a term that we use to refer to beliefs and customs employed by a particular group. When we look at influential figures in our field of study for this lesson, we will have to know the people, places, and events that impacted their lives and their social identities such as race, ethnicity, language, gender, sexual orientation, class, ability, and religion (among others) to surface what influenced their writing and what they influenced in their career and lifetime.

For our reporting about our Spanish writer, tell students that they are going to write a "Something You Should Know" poem about a Spanish writer. The students know what this poem is because they have written one. They also understand how our lived experiences shape who we are and become.

I recommend doing a collaborative poem on one thought leader to model the process.

Gradual Release Lesson

For our Spanish class standard, let us consider I do, Pura Teresa Belpré y Nogueras, Afro-Puerto Rican. Together, *investigate and report on ways in which a writer has influenced or been influenced by historical, social, and cultural issues or events.* First, investigate. Project the chart on the board and invite students to use their school or personal device to research Pura Belpré. Students will quickly discover she was born in Cidra, Puerto Rico, so you may open a map or invite a student to find Cidra, Puerto Rico. Students will also discover that she was born around 1899 and died in 1982.

What was perhaps most influential in Belpré's life was that she was educated, and when she came to New York City for a relative's wedding, she was offered a job at the public library. She was the first Puerto Rican librarian in New York City, and the first to write and promote literature in English and Spanish. This is a great start, but students need to find out what was going on in Puerto Rico in the 1920s that made it possible for Belpré to become a librarian. Was it common for women to go to college? What about her family made that possible? What was going on in the US or New York (NY), and maybe a particular part of NY, at that time that made them ready to hire the first Puerto Rican women librarian? What influenced Belpré to advocate for Spanish literature in the library system? So, students need to look at history and also Belpré's social identities—gender, culture, race, language, ability, and class.

Poetic Pathways to Comprehension ◆ 65

TABLE 3.2 Teacher Inquiry Chart for a Thought Leader: Pura Belpré

	Person	Possibly influenced by			
	Writer city of birth, years of life	Historical events or issues	Social events or issues	Cultural events or issues	Influencer of
Criteria					
We do	Pura Belpré	Jones Act of 1917 granted U.S. citizenship to all Puerto Ricans.	1920s Puerto Rican women migrated to New York (Why)	1920s public library effort to hire ethnically diverse women	First Puerto Rican librarian in NYC
	Cidra, Puerto Rico				
	2/2/1899-7/1/1982	Spanish-American War of 1898, just before Pura was born	Women's rights	Beliefs libraries were "only English"	Traveled NYC telling stories in English and Spanish, which had not been done before
			Multilingual		
		Libraries from private to public	Literacy		Bought Spanish books for the library
		Harlem Renaissance	Economy		

Now, students select a historical figure and create a similar chart.

The next part is to report: *investigate and report on ways in which a writer has influenced or been influenced by historical, social, and cultural issues or events (Table 3.2).* This is where poetry comes in.

Something You Should Know About Pura Belpré by Sarah Donovan

> is that she fell in love with stories at her grandmother's
> feet, listening to animal adventures that she carried from
> Puerto Rico to New York around eighteen. She cut
> cloth and thread needles, weaving stories until hired
> by New York C seeking Spanish-speaking immigrants.
> Literacy was for the upper class before then; public libraries
> were changing. Carnegie's money and Harlem's
>   Renaissance
> sparked cultural shifts. Pura collected Spanish
>   language books,
> helped new immigrants navigate the library, started
>   bilingual story
> time, and wrote the stories she could not find.
> like a cute cockroach folktale and stories that
> honor rural life in Puerto Rico. There is now an
>   award for
> Latino/writers and illustrators who affirm and celebrate
> Latino cultural experiences. Maybe you will read their
> stories, too – maybe you will write a poem for them.

I synthesized facts from my inquiry to write this poem, gathering several resources. Depending on your goals, you could then model how to cite sources with short works cited lessons or endnotes. Still, this poem demonstrates progress in the learning standard in that, I have a chart with my inquiry notes and then I synthesized those notes into this poetic report. We can see some historical influence of the shift from private to public libraries and the Harlem Renaissance, which cultivated incredible arts during that time. We also see how the impact of the Jones Act caused many Puerto Ricans to migrate to the US and how Pura's education in Puerto Rico offered her an opportunity out of the garment factories and into the libraries at a pivotal social and cultural time in the city.

The next step in this is for students to repeat the process by researching another Spanish writer. You can offer a list so that students are researcher writers from the past and present times and from different Spanish-speaking countries and communities. See the list of authors above that can lead to interesting inquiries and a range of poetic reports.

Student Example

One student, whom we will call Julia loves the verse novel *Poet X* by Elizabeth Acevedo and selected her for the project. Here is the student's research notes (Table 3.3):

TABLE 3.3 Student Inquiry Chart for Thought Leader: Elizabeth Acevedo

Historical events or issues	Social events or issues	Cultural events or issues	Influencer of/by...
The Poet X won the National Book Award for Young People's Literature in 2018.	known for Dominican American experiences and diverse voices	traveled to the Dominican Republic, where her mother and her siblings were raised to inspire writing	Naima Coster suggested she write with a candle burning, and that is part of her ritual
With the Fire on High (2019) was named a Michael L. Printz Honor Book and a Pura Belpre Author Honor Book.	advocates for diverse representation in books	Afro-Latinx cultural experiences	discussions on literature to influence high school English teachers
Clap When You Land (2020) focused on identity and family.	famous spoken word artists	heritage of immigrant experiences	influences youth to write poetry

- Acevedo (n.d.). About. Elizabeth Acevedo. www.acevedowrites.com/about
- Reyes, D. (2023, September 7). An interview with Elizabeth Acevedo, 2023 First Novel Prize finalist for *Family Lore*. The Center for Fiction. https://centerforfiction.org/interviews/an-interview-with-elizabeth-acevedo-2023-first-novel-prize-finalist-for-family-lore/

Something You Should Know About Elizabeth Acevedo by Julia

is that she burns a candle when she writes
about immigrant life from the Dominican Republic
to New York, visiting her mother's home
to envision the place that permeates the
pages of her novels, which won awards
and honors like her spoken word
poems that made her *Poet X* so beautiful
in verse (which I love). Perhaps that is why
I want to write poems about my family
maybe tell a story in English and Korean
to show you our family's journey
and maybe win a book honor someday,

How do I Assess Their Learning?

To effectively assess student learning in poetry writing, start by evaluating their understanding of key terms and conceptual goals. This involves checking if students accurately use and reflect on terminology and concepts discussed during lessons. As you observe their work, ensure they draw on reliable evidence from the provided texts to support their writing and ideas. Document this evidence in your grade book, noting how well each student applies the lessons to their poetry.

Perhaps more important is to assess their metacognitive process by inviting a short reflection about their poem. For instance, between her note-taking chart and poem, we can trace Julia's research and synthesis. She understands the cultural influences and influences of Elizabeth Acevedo, and we also see how Acevedo has inspired Julia to become a writer. Students can write a short artist statement, or you can informally confer with students.

Julia's Artist Statement: I enjoyed writing this poem because Elizabeth Acevedo is my favorite author. Ms.

Merkle gave me *Poet X* to read during English class last year, and I was surprised to see that it was in verse form. I have never read a book like that. This activity gave me a chance to learn more about my favorite author and write a poem for her—well, for class.

After years of grading and manipulating rubrics to capture the most important learning, I have found that this scale (in which you can change numbers as needed) best evaluates the finished product or evidence of learning. You enter the key components in the left column. Then, the product either "meets expectations" by reflecting on class lessons, "partially meets" to indicate which aspect of the assignment needs support or more time, or "not attempted" yet (Table 3.4).

TABLE 3.4 Rubric for Something You Should Know Inquiry and Poem about a Thought Leader

Rubric			
Assignment component	*Reflects a strong grasp of concepts and careful attention to detail*	*Partially meets/ revision support*	*Not attempted*
Understanding key terms (e.g., culture, writer) Conceptual goal in notes (e.g., influence) Draws on reliable evidence to inform the poem (e.g., notes, citation) Personal reflection within the poem or in an artist's statement (e.g., can explain the process and rationale)	Thoughtfully completed in a way that reflects class lessons and meets criteria.	The product is only partially developed or it reflects course lessons in a limited way. Revisit class activities and lessons or teacher feedback for further development.	The assignment is missing or incomplete, so it cannot be scored. Alternatively, the product does not reflect the assignment guidelines.

Being Thoughtful About Grading

When I taught 8th grade, I taught six classes for 40 minutes each and had 180 students in one year. I do not advocate that you collect all these poems and grade them; rather, you can evaluate the work as students are developing the assignment and then, once again, when they publish or share these. Create a roster like the one below with each of the components and evaluate as students write so that you can track who needs support and who seems to grasp each concept (Table 3.5). By systematically recording these elements, you can provide targeted feedback and track each student's progress and understanding. This process continues the humanizing work rather than reducing students' learning to points or letter grades too swiftly.

Poetic practice supports students' varied ways of processing as they draw on their prior knowledge and experiences along with the central text. Welcome students' uses of their home languages in their writing, and let students know they can play with the suggested forms and structures. If needed, you can offer a template for greater scaffolding. See Chapter 5 for examples of templates.

If "Something You Should Know" is your first poetry lesson, we suggest you ask students to archive their poems in a folder to build a portfolio for ongoing reflection on learning and the possibility of revising the poem with new perspectives and knowledge.

TABLE 3.5 Roster Chart for Tracking Student Progress

	Understanding key terms in notes	*Conceptual goal in notes*	*Draws on reliable evidence from the "notes" to inform the poem*	*Personal reflection within the poem or in an artist's statement*
Julia	✓	✓	✓	✓
Alex	✓	✓	✓	Missing
Sam	Revision	Revision	Revision	Missing

Publishing

In an assignment like this "Something You Should Know," students will have created many wonderful poems. Some may be about the same thought leader, though we imagine you will be able to find many in your field when you expand your search globally.

We love a gallery walk for publishing the poems and learning from one another. This is also a time you can use for evaluating final products.

For a physical gallery walk, print the poems and tape them around the room. Students can then use sticky notes to write from the ethos, pathos, and logos sentence stems about the new poems. For a digital gallery walk, students can publish their poems on a class discussion board and write comments. We like playing background music and reserving the entire class period for reading and responding to poems.

Extension

A follow-up to this would be for students to look for themes in the lives of these writers. What do they notice about the impact of historical, social, and cultural issues on a writer's life, and how does the writer impact our lives? They could look across the inquiry charts and poems to theorize about causes and effects.

Adapting this Lesson to Other Content Areas

Adapting a lesson on thought leaders to various subject areas involves using poetry to explore the impact of historical, social, and cultural contexts on influential figures. By crafting a poem about a thought leader in history, science, math, English, or other fields, students can concentrate their understanding of how significant issues shaped these individuals' lives and contributions. For example, in a history class, students might write poetry about a historical figure like Nelson Mandela, reflecting on the sociopolitical struggles he faced and his influence on global justice. In a science class, a poem might explore Marie Curie's contributions to chemistry and the impact of her era's gender norms on her work. In math, students could write about a mathematician like Ada Lovelace, considering how her era's technological limitations influenced her pioneering work in computing. Similarly, in fields like CPR and first aid, poetry could help students reflect on the contributions of key figures in medical advancements and the societal needs that drove their innovations. This approach aligns with educational standards that encourage students to investigate and articulate how individuals are influenced by and influence their historical and cultural contexts. By integrating poetry into these explorations, students synthesize information in a creative and concentrated form, deepening their engagement with both the subject matter and the personal dimensions of influential figures.

Sample Lesson - Where I'm From: Natural Hazards

Oklahoma emergency certified educator Joseph was assigned the high school course Environmental Science. The 2020 standards indicate that students should learn to *"construct an explanation based on evidence for how the availability of natural resources, occurrence of natural hazards, and climate changes affect human activity"* (ESS3). To teach this, Joseph might teach that natural hazards can be from interior processes (volcano eruptions, earthquakes), surface processes (tsunamis, landslides, mudslides, and soil erosion), and severe weather (tornados, hurricanes, floods, and droughts).

Before teaching about natural hazards, Joseph could use poetic practice to tap into students' prior knowledge and experience of any number of these natural hazards literally. For example, students in Oklahoma know tornados well and understand that the damage caused to homes and farms has caused families to move. They may be aware of the Popocatépetl Volcano eruption in Mexico (May 2023) and have heard or seen stories of families leaving or families who chose to stay. Students may have seen or heard of the mudslides in California or have family there who were forced to relocate. Another approach is to consider the abstract or figurative. Joseph could ask students to consider how internal or surface emotional eruptions have impacted their relationships with others. All of these are great ideas, but how? How can Joseph engage students in doing this thinking, synthesis, and critical thinking about the effect of natural hazards on human activity?

During: Joseph became a teacher because Oklahoma was struggling to offer a hospitable place for teachers to thrive. With a background in environmental engineering specializing in drought, Joseph was sure to do great with this standard by teaching all he knew about drought. He had a slideshow with various terms (see the vocabulary section). However, he thought the Dust Bowl lecture would be most relevant to his Oklahoma students: *Dust Bowl: An area of the US Plains that included parts of Kansas, Colorado, Oklahoma, Texas, and New Mexico. The term was coined in the 1930s when dry weather and high winds caused many dust storms throughout the United States, particularly in this area.* After his lecture, he gave students a 10-question quiz. Some students did well, but this did not help meet the standard or learning goal of students being able to develop skills to construct an explanation based on his lecture, and students did not have anything to do while they listened to help them see the cause and effect; they were not sure how to engage with the content, so they listened or tried to listen.

After: Knowing what students would do after hearing the lecture or reading the slides is the key to helping them do something during their reading, listening, or viewing, so having a poetic practice in mind as the endpoint would have helped Joseph think about what students might do during the lecture, reading, or viewing.

Inspiration

Today's poetic practice is inspired by poet George Ella Lyon. She suggests we revise lists of what we know into poems by rearranging lines and adding repetition. Her website has many examples of poems from *Where I'm From*, but we will adapt them here for our lesson on natural hazards.

You might say: *Today we are going to learn about natural hazards, and this connects to our lives because of cause and effect. Think about where you are from and how these places, objects, and experiences have made you who you are today.*

Process with Mentor Text

> **Sarah:** *Paste this poem from educator Anna J. Small Roseboro in your physical/digital notebook. As we read this poem, let us look at the cause and effect of her lived experience.*

I'm from Detroit and the sound of Motown
While rhythm and blues beat with "Solid on down"
Gospel and hymn tunes become my solid ground.

I'm from early to bed and early to rise.
If you're good today, maybe you'll get fries
Close that door! Keep out the flies.

I'm from brothers and sisters
From "Yes, Ma'am and Misters"
Skating and falling and getting shin blisters.

I'm from go to school, don't act a fool.
Don't matter at all if you're not thought of as cool,
Some go to church, and some go to shul.

I'm from the Tigers and Lions, GM and Ford
Library cards keep us from getting bored.
Borrowing was all that we could afford.

I'm from family; family is all
When we're together, we have a ball.
On, and yes, my maiden name was Small.

Sarah (continued): *What do you notice? Yes, Michigan is important here, and it seems that with the big family, some rules and routines have kept things organized, maybe even strict. And we see that Anna uses rhyme here to create a rhythm, even some whimsy as she concludes that "family is all." That is the core or heart of where she is from.*

Your Turn

Sarah: *Now that we have a mentor text, we can think about the people, places, and things that show where we are from. I have a template here, or you can work from Anna's poem. Let's take 5 minutes and see what we can do. I am going to write, too. As we write, let's remember our norm of no-walk/no-talk to respect this writing time.*

- I am from (three products that you use, use proper nouns like the brands).
- I am from (people or figures who've impacted who you've become).
- I am from (places that are a comfort for you, that you love to be, that have stories).
- I am from (life events that have impacted you).

As the teacher, you should write a few lines of your poem on the board or if you have a document camera. Students are curious about you and also want to see you valuing the writing process. Then, you can move around the room. The "walk" is actually important for you because this is prime assessment and teaching time. You will see which students get right to it, which are processing, and which may be paralyzed by it, so you have to notice that in the first two minutes so that you can support students as needed. Sometimes all they need is to talk through some ideas. Your role is to pose questions. Be curious

Pair-Share

After five minutes or so, invite students to do a pair share. They can just read what they have to a neighbor. Maybe offer a kind response from the rhetorical triangle:

- Logos: I learned a new fact, which is... Thank you.
- Pathos: When you said X, I felt Y.
- Ethos: You seem to have expertise in... or your writing is great because it was vivid, sensory, and rhythmic.

Again, it is best if you model this first. Read your poem and invite a few students to say something nice to you using the sentence stems.

Sarah: *(You probably want to hear my poem?) Okay, so I have a first draft of my poem. I am going to read it to you. Can I have 2 people respond to show how this might look and feel?*

I am from Johnson & Johnson talcum and Comet scouring powders.
I am from fairy Godmother Jean and the ghost of Grandpa Baiocchi.
I am from the rosebush that never had roses, and fry pans full of imitation meat.
I am from divorced parents, seven sisters, three brothers, and Lucky & Stripe who ate steak.

Student 1: *I want to know more about the ghost!*
Student 2: *And I want to know about that imitation meat.*
Sarah: *Thanks. You can see how the poem drops information but does not tell the whole story. In almost every line, every phrase is a story of the components of who I am, and that is what we are focusing on today, the components in our environment or the natural hazards that develop in environments. But before that, enjoy your pair-share.*

Now for Your Content: Natural Hazards

To begin the lesson, you might say: *As I discuss various natural hazards today during my 15-minute lecture, I'd like you to select a hazard (volcano, tsunami, tornado, mudslide) and consider where it comes from and what impact it has had on people.*

As the content expert, you will have the content knowledge and need to decide the best way to convey or create inquiry around the concept. You might present all the information to students or model how to take notes on one natural hazard, the volcano, and then offer inquiry time for students to research other natural hazards from their textbooks or the internet.

The gradual release model offers a blend of lecture, demonstration, and guided practice that supports students' self-directed learning.

Gradual Release Lesson

For our lesson on natural hazards, let's begin with the volcano. You may create a slide deck with the following details and help students take notes and/or fill in partial notes, depending on their needs (Table 3.6). The key here is that students need content knowledge or "text" to synthesize in poem form to deepen their understanding of the concept.

TABLE 3.6 Class Notes from a Video Lecture on Volcanoes

Natural Hazard: Volcano

Materials it is made from	What causes it to become a hazard?	What is the impact on land?	What is the impact on people?
Magma: Molten rock beneath the Earth's surface. Lava: Magma that reaches the surface. Pyroclastic materials: Ash, volcanic rocks, pumice, and gasses ejected during eruptions. Volcanic gasses: Water vapor, carbon dioxide, sulfur dioxide, hydrogen sulfide, and other gasses released during eruptions.	Eruptions occur when magma, ash, and gasses release from the Earth's crust due to pressure build-up in the magma chamber. Plate tectonics: Movement of the Earth's plates, especially at convergent and divergent boundaries, leads to volcanic activity. Explosive eruptions: When high-pressure gas builds up in viscous magma, the eruption can be highly explosive, releasing ash, lava, and gasses. Lava flows and pyroclastic flows: These fast-moving currents of hot gas and volcanic matter are particularly dangerous, traveling at high speeds.	Destruction of habitats: Lava flows and ash deposition can destroy vegetation and ecosystems. Alteration of landscapes: Volcanoes can create new landforms but also bury existing ones under lava and ash. Soil fertility: Volcanic ash can enhance soil fertility over time, benefiting agriculture in the long term.	Loss of life and property: Explosive eruptions can cause deaths and damage infrastructure (homes, roads, and buildings). Health issues: Volcanic ash can cause respiratory problems and contaminate water supplies. Displacement: People living near active volcanoes may need to evacuate due to impending eruptions or long-term hazards (ashfall, gasses). Economic disruption: Destruction of agricultural land, infrastructure, and tourism industries can lead to significant economic losses. Climate effects: Large volcanic eruptions can inject particles into the atmosphere, potentially leading to short-term global cooling by blocking sunlight.

After the lesson, you might say: *Now that we've learned a little bit about volcanoes, let's write a collaborative poem about the causes and impact. Keep your notes out, and then let's work through this together.* Here is a template:

- I am from (materials).
- I am from (what makes it become a hazard).
- I am from (what is the impact on land).
- I am from (what is the impact on people).

If you have a Smartboard or can project the poem on the board, you can take student suggestions and write together. You can also divide up the four parts of the poem for small groups to write together. Here is an example of what the volcano poem can look like, but if multiple class periods are writing this poem, it will look different each time, which again supports our call to write poems about content rather than doing multiple choice quizzes. Knowledge and learning need space for nuance and synthesis.

Volcano: Where I'm From

I am from gas, lava, and tephra.
I grow from magma moving up
but not erupt-ing like a balloon.
Intrusion.
I grow from eruption, too, magma
Spilling down my mountain adding
To my waistline as it cools,
Becomes crusty.
Extrusion.
I am from the edges of
Tectonic plates
From land
From oceans.

I am from Mount Etna

Showing ash over Sicily
Forcing airports to suspend flights
I am from Popocatépetl
Closing schools in Mexico City.

I am from neighbors
Who return to me
When the ash settles
Hoping for no more extrusion.
Migration is slow where I'm from
Not like landslides.

After the collaborative poem, you might say: *Now that we've learned a little bit about natural hazards, select a hazard, do some research (or use the textbook), and write a poem about the causes and impact.*

Depending on your class, you may have students write in pairs or small groups, but we do like giving students their own quiet inquiry time to bring their voice to the poem and the interaction between the text (notes) and the poem they are creating.

Student Example

One student, whom we will call Alex selected hurricanes. Here is the student's notes (Table 3.7):

TABLE 3.7 Student Notes on Hurricanes

Natural Hazard: Hurricanes

Materials it is made from	What causes it to become a hazard?	What is the impact on land?	What is the impact on people?
warm ocean water; wet air; low-pressure systems; clouds and rain; strong winds	rapid intensification; storm surge; heavy rainfall; high winds; movement and unpredictability	coastal erosion; flooding; damage to ecosystems	loss of life; destruction of property; economic damage; displacement; health risks; power and communication outages

Some instructional sequences end with a graphic organizer. Students fill it out and get graded. The student has taken notes and may have learned some facts about hurricanes, but we need to see that synthesis or understanding of how the student is making sense of the cause and effect of all these components. Of course, we can ask a student to write an essay, and that may be a learning goal, but if knowledge and understanding about natural hazards is the goal (and not essay writing), writing a poem can help students deepen their learning. This is higher-order thinking. We are not assessing the poem here, but what the student does in writing the poem and what the student can say or express about the process.

Here is Alex's poem:

I am from warm ocean water, air, pressure, rain, and
 wind
which together may sound like a typical storm.
But I am also from rapid intensification like
a school year picking up speed and a surge that
pushes volumes of water toward coastal areas.
I am from reshaping those coastlines and lost beaches
from overflowing rivers and flattened forests.
I am from destruction of property with no insurance
from evacuations and disease, medical emergencies
no word of life or death for days after.

How do I Assess Their Learning?

As in the previous lesson on thought leaders, the assessment begins the moment students start taking notes. Your role is to move around the room and support their inquiry process as they gather knowledge about the topic, which includes new terms and the concept of cause and effect. You can teach as you confer with students. You can point to resources and refine their understanding. This process frees you up for individualized and differentiated instruction.

You can list each student's assignment components on your roster and check their progress as you assess their knowledge and understanding (Table 3.8).

In your conferring, you can ask students to reflect on their process: *Tell me what seems most important for you in your notes. How did you include that in your poem? What causes all these elements to become a hazard? Do you know of any examples from the news or your personal experiences?*

Alternatively, you can ask students to write a short reflection or exit slip like Julia's Artist Statement in the previous lesson. Here is what Alex might write, depending on his geographic experiences (e.g., if he lives or has lived in Louisiana or a coastal city).

> Alex's Artist Statement: I was so glad that you let us choose which topic to write about. I read the graphic novel *Drowned City* in class last year and learned a lot about the impact of Hurricane Katrina. However, I didn't learn about the materials or natural situations that make a hurricane out of water, air, wind, etc. I felt terrible about the impact of Katrina and think knowing more about the impact can, at least, put some responses in place.

TABLE 3.8 Rubric for I am From Inquiry and Poem on Natural Hazards

Rubric

Assignment component	Reflects a strong grasp of concepts and careful attention to detail	Partially meets/ revision support	Not attempted
Understanding key terms (e.g., materials, hazard) Conceptual goal in notes (e.g., impact on land and people) Draws on reliable evidence to inform the poem (e.g., notes) Personal reflection within the poem or in an artist's statement (e.g., can explain the process, and rationale)	Thoughtfully completed in a way that reflects class lessons and meets criteria.	The product is only partially developed or it reflects course lessons in a limited way. Revisit class activities and lessons or teacher feedback for further development.	The assignment is missing or incomplete to a degree that it is not able to be scored. Or the product does not reflect the assignment guidelines.

Publishing in an Open Mic

We love an open mic for students to practice formal public speaking and share what they learned with the class. Even if multiple students write poems about hurricanes, their poems will be different, and there is much to learn.

To prepare, have students practice reading their poems aloud with a partner using our VEEPPP resource (Table 3.9). This supports students in practicing volume, eye contact, expression, pace, pronunciation, and professionalism. In addition to practicing, I ask for two volunteers to be MCs or to host the open mic. Their job is to introduce the poets and to facilitate the compliments.

TABLE 3.9 Public Speaking Guide: VEEPPP

VEEPP	*Public Speaking*
Volume	We can hear you in the back of the room. You may make your voice louder or softer in certain parts to emphasize something, show passion/emotion, or make the audience lean in, but it is related to content. Your volume does not distract from your message.
Eye Contact	We can see your eyes at different points of the performance, which shows that you are trying to connect with your audience. You can also hold eye contact from three angles of the room, which shows that you know your content well.
Expression	The way you say the words and phrases shows how you interpret the mood and content to communicate to the audience. You may change your expression in different parts as the mood shifts or ideas become more serious or light-hearted.
Pace	You stay within the time allowed. You perform with a pace that matches the content and mood: slow enough for us to hear and process the words and fast enough for us to feel the rhythm. You may slow down to emphasize certain parts or to let an important idea really resonate with the audience.
Pronunciation	You practiced and know the words you have written, especially technical ones. The audience is not distracted by phrasing or unclear pronunciation.
Professionalism	You prepared for the performance. You stand strong (no swaying), say "thank you" at the end to signal closure, stay for a moment to accept the applause, and your demeanor treat the topic and audience with respect.

Supporting the Listeners

After the poets read their poems, the listeners/audience write a compliment for the poet using ethos, pathos, logos, and sentence stems. This is just to promote engaged listening, a learning standard that needs intentional practice (Table 3.10).

TABLE 3.10 Listening Sheet

Name	Feature to Celebrate	Text Evidence
1. Sarah	Sensory language – **smell**	"rotting stench of a fish left in the garbage for days"
2.		
3.		
4.		

Perhaps more important than listening and noticing is the applause and compliments. The emcees should invite at least two compliments from the class after each poem is read aloud.

Adapting this Lesson to Other Content Areas

In any content area, there are concepts of cause and effect, issues that have implications for various stakeholders. We also know that most content areas have some learning standard related to multimodal literacy, and graphs broadly and infographics specifically can be applicable in many content areas. You could use this Maths lesson to review graphs and charts in your content area or modify it to invite students to write about the places you are studying in history, English language arts, science, and others. We invite you to collaborate in your professional learning communities to consider the concepts in your content area that you can draw on to adapt this lesson for your classroom. Trust us when we say you will find much joy in reading your students' poems about their origins.

Sample Lesson: X Tells Me to be Discrete or Continuous

Today's poetic practice is inspired by Dr. Chea Parton. Depending on where and how you grew up, you likely find that there are certain expectations of being in that place and then contrast when you are in new or unfamiliar environments, sometimes or most times because of expectations. This is because people in a certain place (geographically like the north or south or locally like private or public spaces) bring expectations or, for today's inspiration "tell you a way to be."

Inspiration

To launch the lesson, you may say: *Today in Algebra 1 we are going to uncover and explore Standard A1.D.1 Display, describe, and compare data. For linear relationships, make predictions and assess the reliability of those predictions. Specifically, we are going to interpret graphs as being discrete or continuous. I want you to think about what data tells a graph to be: discrete or continuous. First, let's think about what data in your life tells you to be you.*

Process With Mentor Text

Sarah   Open your notebooks to a fresh page and paste the mentor text from Dr. Chea Parton into it.

Place and the Possible Me(s) by Chea Parton

The cornfields tell me to be
small
The stalks envelop me in their greenery
But they also tell me to be
resilient.

The Mill Street tells me to be
friendly
To visit the farmer table and say hello
I know pretty much everybody in there
So it also tells me to be
guarded.

Home tells me to
speak my mind
Ideas
are paramount
And
school grammar
Don't matter
And honestly
Ain't preferable.

School tells me Home is
dumb
uneducated
School listens more to the
Words as I say them
Than the
ideas
The words create.

I listen and
I hear it all.
Whether I want to
or not

It all becomes part of me
And I believe it all
Until I won't
I follow the rules
Until I don't

I decide to be the
Me
I want to be

But place has still shown what
Me
Is
Possible.

Sarah: Chea writes, "The cornfields tell me to be/small/The stalks envelop me in their greenery/But they also tell me to be/resilient." *Her family farmed corn in Indiana, and she has clearly learned some things from the land.*

Your Turn

Sarah: Think about a place important to you and what it tells you to be. I can think of many places. I have lived in Illinois, Florida, and Oklahoma. I have lived in suburbs and cities and beaches. I have lived in very tiny rooms with plywood for walls and large rooms held up by bricks and high ceilings. For me now, it is the road beside my new home in Oklahoma that is telling me to embrace the country, so in my notebook, I am going to write "Richmond Road tells me to be." Now tell your elbow partner what you will write about. Okay, let us take 5 minutes and see what we can do. What does all the data of this place tell us to be? I am going to write, too. As we write, let's remember our norm of no-walk/no-talk to respect this writing time.

Now that this is our third time working through the routine of writing poetry together, you know the routine. Start writing. Then, a few minutes in, stop and look around. Visit with students who may need some support. Respond from a place of curiosity, asking them to think about the places they spend time in and what the objects there tell us to be: loud, quiet, active, calm, playful, serious, big, small, etc.

Pair-Share

After five minutes or so, invite students to do a pair share. They can just read what they have to a neighbor. Maybe offer a kind response from the rhetorical triangle:

- Logos: I learned a new fact, which is… Thank you.
- Pathos: When you said X, I felt Y.
- Ethos: You seem to have expertise in… or your writing is great because it was vivid, sensory, and rhythmic.

Again, it is best if you model this first. Read your poem and invite a few students to say something nice to you using the sentence stems.

Sarah: *(You probably want to hear my poem?) Okay, so I have a first draft of my poem. I am going to read it to you. Can I have 2 people respond to show how this might look and feel?*

Richmond Road tells me to be
quiet in the dust of the pickup trucks
to step into the wake and wave my hand
hello to the tractor that comes next.

The vulture hovering above the road
kill of Raccoon or is it Armadillo tells
me to walk on by; there's nothing to see
here on this road.

Student 1: *I learned you live on a busy road; I bet your car is dusty, too!*

Student 2: *When you said, "There's nothing to see here," I could see that vulture being like a mobster or something. It is also kind of funny.*

Sarah: *Thanks. So now, you will do that for each other. Remember to receive your compliment with a "thanks."*

Now for Your Content: Discrete and Continuous Graphs

You are the content area expert, so you know all about graphs. Moreover, you know your students and learning context. There are many ways to introduce a concept. Each way will be effective for some students and less effective for others.

Lecturing may be great for motivated students but not for students who prefer activity. A demonstration lesson is a lot like a think-aloud. They may enjoy watching you puzzle through a problem or show the steps to complete an activity. However, some students may want to proceed at their own pace and disengage halfway through a demo. Guided practice is the focus we have used in this chapter (e.g., the gradual release lesson). This teaching method blends lecture and demonstration but turns over the activity to students who need to get their hands on the problem, resources, and materials. The partner and independent practice frees you up to move around the room for individualized instruction, differentiating or modifying in the moment students need support. Finally, you might try recording a lecture or demonstration for students to be able to control (stop and start) the video as they take notes, try an activity, or work with a partner to solve a problem. The recording makes learning more self-guided, but you are entirely free to do small group lessons or individualized instruction with students who need it.

Whatever you decide for this lesson, you may offer a graphic organizer for students to paste into their paper or digital notebook so that they can have the key vocabulary and conceptual information to refer back to through the lesson and the larger unit. Remember that comprehension is not in the recall of facts but in understanding the relationship of terms and concepts. Writing a poem supports students in synthesizing information and meaning-making in relationship to their own prior learning and experiences.

Let's say you go with the video, you might say: *As you watch this video about discrete and continuous graphs, think about what data tells the graph to be. Open your notebook to take notes. As you watch the video and take notes, I will move around the room with some graphs and help you apply the notes to a few examples* (Table 3.11).

TABLE 3.11 Discrete and Continuous Data Note-Taking

	Types of data	*The graph looks like*	*How I can interpret the meaning of the data*
discrete	countable quantities like number of students in class, number of books, number of goals scored in a futbol match; whole numbers (no half students); examples like test scores, number of phones sold, survey results like yes/no or number of pets in your home	bar graphs: each category has its own bar; the height represents the counts pie chart: each slice is a category in a size related to the count line/dot plots: data points plotted on a number line to show frequency or count	noticing trends; making comparisons bar graph: if one bar is taller than another; it shows that category is more common or greater pie chart: larger slices indicate the more common category plots: the spread or cluster of the data indicates a more frequent value
continuous	measurable values that can have decimals and fractions like height, weight, temperature, time, distances; can be precise	histograms: bars represent ranges; the bars are touching because the data is continuous across ranges; line graphs: show data over time; connection of data points with lines box plots: summarize data using median, quartiles, outliers scatter plots: show the relationship between 2 variables	each bar represents a range of values, not specific numbers; interpret how a variable changes over time or with other variables if the line goes up or down; interpret the relationship between variables like positive (up) or negative (down) trends; deeper insight into change because of its measurable non-discrete nature

After the lesson, you might say: *Now that we've learned a little bit about discrete and continuous data. Let's think about the things that are important to us—whether they are countable and whole like your pets or measurable like the size of your cell phone screens. Think back to the poem you wrote about how a place tells you to be. What is countable and measurable in that place would, thus, tell the graph to be either discrete or continuous. Write a poem about the data that tells the graph to be discrete or continuous. You may need to revisit the video and use your notes.*

Student Example

One student, whom we will call Sam selected *discrete*. Here is Sam's poem. As you read Sam's poem, assess his understanding of the vocabulary and concept in addition to how Sam is synthesizing that information with what he knows and cares about:

Discrete: This X Tells Me to Be

> The data tells the graph to be
> discrete.
> The points are separate and distinct–
> the points are not connected.
> They can't be.
> The number of people in this school
> is a whole number.
> People can be fractured by harm
> but cannot be a fraction of worth.
> The days I count until I
> see my grandmother (and get Christmas
> presents) tell the graph to be
> discrete. Though I will not be --
> I love presents.
> Yesterday was a snowstorm, I stayed
> home to play; can we count the snowflakes?
> Today is pizza day, everyone
> came to school.
> The date (and the weather and what's for lunch)

tells the graph what to be, which just might
improve attendance
I think I'd prefer living in a discrete graph;
I don't like weighing myself.

What do you notice about Sam's understanding of discrete and continuous data and the way that data tells a graph to be? What do you notice about Sam as a learner and as a person?

We love including a pair-share after students have a draft of the poem. Encourage them to use the ethos, pathos, and logos feedback and even look at the rubric to make revisions. The RADAR (Hurtado, 2012) method is a wonderful resource to offer students in revising their poems:

- Replace words that are not specific, overused, or unclear like pronouns
- Add new information, descriptive words like adjectives or figurative language
- Delete unrelated ideas, sentences, or phrases that distract from the central idea; repeated words or phrases; and
- Reorder so that the important ideas are repeated, build up toward the end, make better sense, logical in sequence

To encourage revision, you can ask students to use a different color pencil or digital color to indicate the changes they made after the peer conferencing and how that impacted their understanding of the key concepts.

How do I Assess Their Learning?

As in the previous lessons on thought leaders and natural hazards, assessment begins with the personal poem and continues through notetaking into the poem writing. Your role is to move around the room and support their inquiry process as they gather knowledge about the topic, which includes new terms and the concept of cause and effect. You can teach as you confer with students. You can point to resources and refine their understanding. This process frees you up for individualized and differentiated instruction (Table 3.12).

On your roster, you can list each student's assignment components and check off their progress as you assess their knowledge and understanding.

In your conferring, you can ask students to reflect on their process: *Tell me what seems most important for you in your notes. How did you include that in your poem? What component was essential to your understanding?*

Or you can ask students to write a short reflection or exit slip like Alex's Artist Statement in the previous lesson. Here is what Sam might write:

Sam's Artist Statement: *I struggle with math, but I am good at writing, so this was a good day for me in class. I liked thinking about the snow day and pizza day. I really miss my grandma because she moved to Florida last year. Now I only see her at Christmas. Julia gave me an idea to add the last two lines about what kind of graph I'd like to be. That was a good addition, I think.*

TABLE 3.12 Rubric for Discrete and Continuous Data Inquiry and Poem

Rubric			
Assignment component	*Reflects a strong grasp of concepts and careful attention to detail*	*Partially meets/ revision support*	*Not attempted*
Understanding key terms (e.g., discrete, continuous) Conceptual goal in notes (e.g., graph reading) Draws on reliable evidence to inform the poem (e.g., notes) Personal reflection within the poem or in an artist's statement (e.g., can explain the process, and rationale)	Thoughtfully completed in a way that reflects class lessons and meets criteria.	The product is only partially developed or it reflects course lessons in a limited way. Revisit class activities and lessons or teacher feedback for further development.	The assignment is missing or incomplete to a degree that it is not able to be scored. Or the product does not reflect the assignment guidelines.

Publishing in a Read-Around

In this chapter, we have offered two other sharing opportunities: gallery walks and open mics. Any publishing method works, can be used multiple times, or can be modified as you determine what your learning community needs.

You do not need a formal publishing of all poems students write, and we hope they will write many. Still, there does need to be some submission process, and that always feels more authentic if someone other than the teacher is reading the poem. Students take greater care when they know someone will learn from them (cognitive) or enjoy their writing (affective), and we want to offer opportunities for community building in class. This idea is adapted from a National Writing Project workshop. You can have students gather in a small group and do a read-around. Here are the instructions:

1. Take out a piece of loose-leaf paper.
2. Take a seat in the circle with the poem.
3. Write the names of peers in the order they are sitting.
4. Each person reads aloud their poem.
5. After each poem, take 30 seconds to write down something that you liked about that poem (its content, its language, how it was constructed, etc.).
6. Now, after everyone has read, pass the loose-leaf paper to one person to the right. Students find their names and read what someone wrote about their poem.
7. Then quickly pass that paper on and repeat.
8. When students get back to their loose-leaf paper, take a few minutes to jot down the feedback you received on your poem.
9. Discuss or write a note about what you already knew, and what surprised you. Think about what you liked in other writers' work.

During this time, your role is to observe and support the process. Afterward, you can debrief the experience and offer students more time to revise their poems and refine their understanding of concepts.

Adapting the Lesson for Other Content Areas

Any element of this lesson can be adapted or excerpted for a different lesson. Create a different graphic organizer where students can gather the key vocabulary and conceptual information. Trade out the "Something You Should Know" for the "Place Tells Me to Be." Use the rubric in an entirely different lesson. Consider using a poem from one of the other chapters in place of the ones offered here. The more you work with this lesson structure of writing a personal poem, extending the idea to a concept, learning the vocabulary and concept, and rendering a new poem to synthesize content and lived experiences, the deeper the learning will be. This is all higher-order thinking and a fully humanizing way of teaching and learning across content areas.

Reflections on Poetry and Comprehension

Poetry writing is a form of place-based writing as it involves the places of the students' lives and lived experiences and the places important to the content area (Azano, 2011; Parton, 2022b). Comprehension assessment that involves writing poetry centers the learner—the learner's cultures, identities, experiences, and perspectives. The poem forms offered here surface transformative people and places in the learners' lives that help teachers be responsive in their teaching. Teachers need access to learners' experiences because this values prior living and learning to inform how we, as teachers, interact with the new knowledge and information students show us during assessment. We need time and space in the classroom to watch students make sense, to be able to sit alongside them, and be curious. To uncover misinterpretation in the moment so that we can reteach, offer a new resource, and refine learning.

References

Acevedo, E. (n.d.). *About*. Elizabeth Acevedo. www.acevedowrites.com/about

Applebee, A. N., Langer, J. A., Nystrand, M., & Gamoran, A. (2003). Discussion-based approaches to developing understanding: Classroom instruction and student performance in middle and high school English. *American Educational Research Journal, 40*(3), 685–730. https://doi.org/10.3102/00028312040003685

Azano, A. (2011). The possibility of place: One teacher's use of place-based instruction for English students in a rural high school. *Journal of Research in Rural Education, 26,* 1–12.

Beck, I. L., & McKeown, M. G. (2006). *Improving comprehension with questioning the author: A fresh and expanded view of a powerful approach*. Scholastic.

Benigni, R. (Director). (1997). *Life is beautiful* [Film]. Miramax Films.

Brown, D. (2015). *Drowned city: Hurricane Katrina and New Orleans*. Clarion Books.

Bunting, E. (1980). *Terrible things: An allegory of the Holocaust*. Jewish Publication Society.

Cook, M. P., & Bennett, C. M. (2022). The cognitive and emotional benefits of poetry writing: Implications for teaching and learning. *Journal of Creative Behavior, 56*(2), 362–375.

Carnegie Council on Advancing Adolescent Literacy. (2010). *Time to act: An agenda for advancing adolescent literacy for college and career success*. Carnegie Corporation of New York.

Eva-Wood, A. L. (2009). Does feeling come first? How poetry can help readers broaden their understanding of metacognition. *Journal of Adolescent & Adult Literacy, 51*(7), 564–576. https://ila.onlinelibrary.wiley.com/doi/10.1598/JAAL.51.7.4

Gajria, M., Jitendra, A., Sacks, S., & Sood, S. (2007). Improving content area instruction for students with learning disabilities: A meta-analysis. *The Journal of Learning Disabilities, 40,* 210–225. https://doi.org/10.1177/00222194070400030301

Gersten, R., Baker, S. K., Smith-Johnson, J., Dimino, J., & Peterson, A. (2006). Eyes on the prize: Teaching complex historical content to middle school students with learning disabilities. *Exceptional Children, 72*(3), 264–280.

Hanauer, D. I. (2010). *Poetry as research: Exploring second language poetry writing*. John Benjamins.

Hanauer, D. I. (2012). Meaningful literacy: Writing poetry in the language classroom. *Language Teaching, 45*(1), 105–115.

Heller, R., & Greenleaf, C. L. (2007). *Literacy instruction in the content areas: Getting to the core of middle and high school improvement*. Alliance for Excellent Education. https://doi.org/10.1177/001440290607200301

Huey, E. B. (1908). *The psychology and pedagogy of reading*. Macmillan.

Hurtado, R. (2012). *Writing coach: Writing and grammar for the 21st century*. Pearson.

Kamil, M. L., Borman, G. D., Dole, J., Kral, C. C., Salinger, T., & Torgesen, J. (2008). *Improving adolescent literacy: Effective classroom and intervention practices* (NCEE 2008-4027). National Center for Education Evaluation and Regional Assistance.

Langer, S. K. (1979). *Philosophy in a new key: A study in the symbolism of reason, rite, and art*. Harvard University Press.

Latinos in Kid Lit. (n.d.). *Pura Belpré award winners*. https://latinosinkidlit.com/pura-belpre-award-winners/HarvardUniversityPress.

Lyon, G. E. (n.d.). *Where I'm from: A writing template*. George Ella Lyon. www.georgeellalyon.com/where.html

Ofsted. 2007. *Poetry in Schools: A Survey of Practice*. Ofsted. http://dera.ioe.ac.uk/7075/8/Poetry_in_schools_(PDF_format)_Redacted.pdf

Parton, C. (2022a, April 17). *Place and the possible me(s)*. Ethical ELA. www.ethicalela.com/15423-2/

Parton, C. (2022b). Who we are where we are: Reading and teaching YAL through a place-based lens. In S. Bickmore, T. H. Strickland, & S. Graber (Eds.), *How young adult literature gets taught* (pp. 141–157). Routledge.

Piaget, J. (1952). *The origins of intelligence in children* (M. Cook, Trans.). International Universities Press.

REFORMA: The National Association to Promote Library and Information Services to Latinos and the Spanish Speaking. (n.d.). *Home*. www.reforma.org/

Reyes, D. (2023, September 7). *An interview with Elizabeth Acevedo, 2023 First Novel Prize finalist for Family Lore*. The Center for Fiction. https://centerforfiction.org/interviews/an-interview-with-elizabeth-acevedo-2023-first-novel-prize-finalist-for-family-lore/

Rosenblatt, L. M. (1938). *Literature as exploration*. D. Appleton-Century.

Smith, C. (n.d.). *Something you should know*. American Poetry Review. https://aprweb.org/poems/something-you-should-know

Swanson, E., Solis, M., Ciullo, S., & McKenna, J. W. (2012). Special education teachers' perceptions and instructional practices in response to intervention implementation. *Learning Disability Quarterly*, *35*(2), 115–126.

Vaughn, S., Roberts, G., Swanson, E. A., Wanzek, J., Fall, A. M., & Stillman-Spisak, S. J. (2015). Improving middle-school students' knowledge and comprehension in social studies: A replication. *Educational Psychology Review*, *27*(1), 31–50. https://doi.org/10.1007/s10648-014-9274-2

Vaughn, S., Swanson, E. A., Roberts, G., Wanzek, J., StillmanSpisak, S. J., Solis, M., & Simmons, D. (2013). Improving reading comprehension and social studies knowledge in middle school. *Reading Research Quarterly*, *48*(1), 77–93.

Vygotsky, L. S. (1978). *Mind in society: The development of higher psychological processes* (M. Cole, V. John-Steiner, S. Scribner, & E. Souberman, Eds. & Trans.). Harvard University Press.

Wiesel, E. (2006). *Night* (M. Wiesel, Trans.). Hill and Wang.

Wineburg, S. (2001). *Historical thinking and other unnatural acts: Charting the future of teaching the past*. Temple University Press.

4

Creative Inquiry
The Heart of Learning

Barbara Edler

Classrooms are filled with a unique combination of individuals with varied interests, backgrounds, and skill sets. Providing them with the tools they need to challenge themselves personally is essential because we want our students to grow as learners rather than sit at a standstill. Students need time to practice in a safe and welcoming space that is the heart of a thriving classroom. To establish a humanizing learning environment that focuses on student growth, we should encourage our pupils to personalize their learning targets and to take ownership of their progress by self-assessing their accomplishments. When students are the center of a classroom, they flourish.

Centering students' lives is especially vital when engaging students with inquiry activities. Student choice is the heart of engagement because it allows them to personalize their educational goals, take ownership of their work, and explore their self-interests. When students have a choice and the opportunity to formulate their direction, they will be more invested in actively pursuing new knowledge and retain interest in their work.

It is also essential to have students develop lines of inquiry about learning and their processes. Encourage them to think deeply about their efforts. For example, regularly ask students to answer the following questions:

- What are you learning?
- How are you learning?
- How can you apply your knowledge?
- How can you connect your knowledge to other areas of study or life?
- What misconceptions or problems did you encounter as you were learning?
- How did you solve the problems you encountered?
- What questions do you have now?

Each of these questions will help students self-assess and reflect on their progress. They will become better able to articulate what they want to learn and how they attained specific skills and information. Continually asking students to answer reflective questions will increase their comprehension, engagement, and attainment of new knowledge. Educators love to see students questioning their texts and the world around them. They love to hear their students ask questions that lead to rich discoveries, and they love to see a student light up when sharing a nugget of information.

Of course, students need guidance as they begin any inquiry activity. Model for students how to set goals, identify what they have learned, and reflect on their triumphs and struggles. They will also need timely, effective feedback that is clear, constructive, and actionable. When students receive feedback while writing and working through the ideas or messages they want to communicate, they can take immediate action and ask new questions for clarification.

Providing input during the moment is far more accessible when the writing is short and focused. This is one reason writing poetry is an effective way to assess a student's knowledge formatively: it offers an accessible, time-sensitive practice for students to learn and receive feedback, especially when they can see ongoing evidence of their learning. Students will miss many learning opportunities if they have to wait until the end of a project to ask questions for clarification.

As a language arts instructor, my students were constantly searching for information. I wanted to activate my students' prior knowledge and have them continue exploring their questions about their interests. To demonstrate their understanding, I offered them a variety of ways to showcase it to me, their peers, and other audiences. Writing creatively was one of my favorite methods to encourage students to present their learning. Creative writing allowed my students to develop their unique voices and insights by writing a brief narrative, a dialogue, a skit, a podcast, or a poem.

In this chapter, I will share ways I used creative writing prompts to help students acquire new knowledge, articulate what they have learned, and showcase the knowledge they possess. In each activity, I began the class with questions that would generate writing ideas, modeled ways to approach the writing task, and provided time for students to draft. Near the end of each period, I closed with reflective activities, allowing students to receive feedback before leaving the classroom. You will immediately see how inquiry is the heart of research and poetry. See Table 4.1 for a glance at ways to use three days.

TABLE 4.1 Overview of Poetic Activities

Class One Exercise *Pre-Research Steps and Building Background Knowledge. Writing Prompt "Twenty Questions"*	**Class Two Exercise** *Taking Notes. Writing Prompt "News & New"*	**Class Three Exercise** *The Final Product. Writing Prompt "Capturing Voices from the Past?"*
1. Searching (15-20 minutes)	1. Note-taking (15-30 minutes)	1. Summative reflecting (5 minutes)
2. Introducing the poetry prompt (10 minutes) to generate questions	2. Introducing the poetry prompt (10 minutes) to dig into sources	2. Introducing the poetry prompt of choices(10 minutes
3. Drafting a poem (15-20 minutes)	3. Drafting (15-30 minutes)	3. Drafting (15-20 minutes)
4. Activity: Pair-sharing or Exit slip	4. Activity: Socratic seminar-ing (10 minutes)	4. Activity: Gallery walking (5-10 minutes)
Outcome: Generating research questions	Outcome: Citing source words	Outcome: Sharing and learning from research

Inquiry is the Heart of Learning

Seeing students make connections and personalize their learning is truly a joy to witness. No matter the subject, book, or skill, I hope my students will embrace it as their own. Inquiry is at the heart of education, so I do what I can to pique my students' interests. I want them to dig deep into the content and reflect on what they have learned and accomplished. In my classroom, research activities continually occur throughout the year, whether it be a focused dive into a particular time, place, or person or an extended activity to expand their depth of knowledge. One of the key reasons I want my students to research is to understand a subject they will be exploring better. Building a student's background knowledge is essential for increasing their own understanding and erasing previous misconceptions.

When I begin a unit where students need to access and build prior knowledge, I do various things to capture their interests. Sometimes, I might show them a photograph of a particular event they may not know much about, as Anna described in Chapter Two. I suggest sharing a short video or a questionnaire to assess what they know, what they think they know, and what they want to know. For example, I might ask, "What do you know about the Civil Rights Movement?" or "What issue would you fight tooth and nail for to create change?" I also play music or show artifacts from a particular era to inspire a better understanding of that time period. I often ask students to write their thoughts about topics before we begin any activity to increase their ability to articulate their ideas and help them connect to their own lives.

You might do any or all of these things because you want/need to know what they know so you can help them extend that information to new learning. Building on the students' knowledge is sound practice.

This chapter offers lessons on using poetry across content areas. As stated in other chapters, you are the content area expert or know how to research the content. I will use a general framework followed by a close look at a science classroom. You can see your content paralleling what I share here. You might have a topic in science, such as Newton's Laws of Motion, which was introduced in middle school, but you can now build on their knowledge for greater nuance and depth. Perhaps the research project you have in mind for students is to make Newton's laws relevant to something in their lives. You might have a topic in mathematics, such as Bayes' Rule, which is crucial to modern statistics. You might even want students to do a research project using a Bayesian model to predict the probability distribution of basketball performance statistics.

Teaching about the Civil Rights Movement was always invigorating in my 11th-grade English/Literature class. Many students knew little about that riveting time of unrest and turmoil. When I taught this unit, I would often provide some background knowledge with short stories, vignettes, and a list of significant events such as Freedom Summer, Montgomery Bus Strike, Emmet Till, etc. I often used a variety of books to help guide students' choice of a particular topic they might wish to explore, such as Diane McWhorter's book *A Dream of Freedom: The Civil Rights Movement from 1964 to 1968*, which provides an excellent overview of critical moments and leaders from this time period. Sharing a quick overview of the book introduced students to several issues, people, and events. I then invited students to plunge deeper into this movement so they would better understand the literature and the impact of social injustice.

The main objective was to focus on one topic to investigate. Secondly, I wanted students to share this newfound knowledge with their peers. If students know they are going to have an audience who will be listening and taking notes, they will be more conscientious of their role within their learning community. Students prepared podcasts, videos, skits, and poems, which they shared in small and large groups, extending everyone's awareness of this movement.

The poetry ideas I share here are for you to use throughout your unit. Think of poetry writing as a tool to expand what works and provide students with more opportunities to write and demonstrate their knowledge.

Writing Poetry as Inquiry

So, why should I ask students to write poetry? How is this even a concept? You might think, "Writing poetry is difficult; students will groan, and I do not know how to evaluate their poems." These are viable doubts, but consider how valuable writing poems can be during any exploratory activity. Writing verse can give students a unique way to engage with their text. It allows them to tap into their creativity and the freedom to express themselves. Students will be better able to receive immediate feedback from their peers and instructors. Furthermore, while assigning poetry writing may seem to be a stretch for many teachers, providing poetry formats and writing with students can show them how to genuinely and meaningfully verify their knowledge of what they have read.

How Does Writing Poetry Synthesize Research?

Using poetry is the perfect format to synthesize the students' knowledge. Poetry is often compact, delivering ideas, emotions, and images in short lines that go straight to the point or heart of the matter. Having students write poetry to exhibit their knowledge will lead them to glean the most important aspects of their subject. More importantly, it will help students use their authentic voice, reducing the temptation to copy and paste information, a method students often employ when writing. Assigning poetry writing can also help instructors and peers share their knowledge and process quickly because the writing will be more focused and compact.

Although writing poetry might seem daunting or questionable, think about it. Students can write a poem fairly quickly to show their perspective, process, and understanding. Writing helps students connect with what they are learning; it provides the student with immediate ownership and makes the learning process visible to both the student and the teacher. It is truly a marvelous approach to presenting knowledge. Providing choices and modeling the writing for them will further enhance these lessons. Plus, writing poetry can be entertaining.

In the next section, I walk you through a specific example of how to use writing poetry with inquiry so that you can assess each step of the process. Then, I break down the three lessons step-by-step. We know that some people benefit from seeing an example first, while others prefer to learn how to do something before seeing an example. If you prefer to see the lessons first, skip down to that section. In other words, you can read this chapter in the order that works for you. "In Practice" takes you into three classrooms: Freshman English, Advanced Science, and First Aid. There are very different classrooms and content; all use writing poetry for learning and assessment.

The three lessons that follow "In Practice" illustrate a step-to-step approach to providing a meaningful research activity that involves writing poetry. Students write poems to show their new knowledge and understanding of the topic. This method of formative assessment allows students to use their creativity and to think more deeply about the information they are gleaning. Students can also self-assess and track their progress, establishing them as responsible learners. Allowing students to write about what they are learning further enables them to maintain the information they are exploring. The formative assessments and self-assessment create a fluent process that makes it easy for the teacher to gauge students' engagement level and quickly respond to the students' misunderstandings and questions as they are immersed in the inquiry process.

Working With Teachers Across the Curriculum

To illustrate the potential for writing poems as a formative assessment, I called on former colleagues to implement my research ideas. Luckily, I was able to visit three different classrooms that were all at various stages of learning. I visited Rex Muston's first-year English classes when the students were beginning a literature unit about surviving tremendous difficulties, Kim Pfeiferling's Advanced Science class, where students were showing their knowledge of biomolecules, and Jessica Koehler's First Aid class, where students were completing a unit on Cardiopulmonary Resuscitation and Automated External Defibrillator.

To prepare, I created presentations to help students follow my instructions and to provide them with mentor texts and models of poetry forms. Slideshows are easily uploaded to an online learning platform such as Schoology Learning or Google Classroom, which is advantageous for absent students.

Sample Lesson: English Language Arts Survivor Stories

Mr. Muston wanted me to visit all of his classes on Monday. He began the class by reviewing the material for the week, and then I took over.

1. I began the exercise with an open-ended question, or "Big Idea:" What does it mean to be a survivor? A discussion ensued.
2. I followed this with a list of websites I prepared on one of the slides, shown in the photograph below. Each of these topics provided a seed for a larger research project around the theme of survival, Mr. Muston's literature unit, which included nonfiction and fictional pieces such as Jack London's short story "To Build a Fire."
3. I explained that they could also choose to do their search about a particular topic not included in the list of links, and we brainstormed and discussed other events to activate further areas of interest. For example, we discussed survivor stories from history, including the sinking of the Titanic and the grisly survival story of The Donner Pass (Andrews, 2024). However, since Mr. Muston had uploaded my presentation to his Google classroom, most students used one of the links to search for a survival story that interested them (Figure 4.1).

Search for a survivor's story. Choose one of these links or do your own online search.

13 People Who Survived The Unsurvivable (buzzfeed.com)	People Who Survived Unimaginable Circumstances (insider.com)
Famous Real Life Survival Stories | Sky HISTORY TV Channel	Concentration Camp Survivors Share Their Stories - The Holocaust | IWM
10 of History's Most Amazing Survival Stories (mentalfloss.com)	Tornado Survivor Stories (weather.gov)
25 Last Survivors Of Exceptionally Significant Historical Events (list25.com)	I was tested to the limit — Rwanda genocide survivor | Africa Renewal (un.org)
10 People Who Survived the Impossible | MapQuest Travel	Survivors of 1972 Uruguay plane crash revisit their tale of going to the extremes to live - ABC News
https://www.scoopwhoop.com/world/last-survivors-historic-events/	12 Incredible Stories of People Who Survived the Impossible - Awareness Act

FIGURE 4.1 List of links students could access to find a survivor story.

4. I then illustrated how to use "Another Kind of Outline," a graphic organizer from Beers and Howell's (2003) book *Reading Strategies for the Content Area, Vol. 1,* to take notes as they read (p.191). I encouraged them to choose specific lines from the texts that would show the critical points of the survivor's story (Table 4.2). My instructions were simple and direct: *As you read your chosen article, highlight essential parts or record notes about your topic.*

TABLE 4.2 Sample Notes to Turn Into a Poem

Big Idea	*Titanic's Last Living Survivor*
• Detail • Detail • Detail • Detail	• Elizabeth Gladys 'Millvina' Dean • Died May 31, 2009 • Sailed with her parents, 3rd class • 2 months & 13 days • The youngest survivor • Only 56 out of 109 children survived

Students had their own Chromebooks, and although some needed to borrow cords to charge their devices or wanted to move to work beside a friend, they could stay on task while reading and sharing information about their online discoveries.

5. Students read and took notes for 20 minutes. I then presented Jim Moore's poem "Twenty Questions" (See Lesson One). I explained to students that they could write about their questions about their survivor's situation. I also encouraged them to put themselves in the survivor's shoes to capture the survivor's situation. I provided the prompt and my own sample poem to illustrate my approach to the poetry prompt (see Figure 4.2).

> Review your notes and write a poem based on your findings. To begin, Read Jim Moore's poem "Twenty Questions."
>
> Reflect on what you learned about a survivor in the article you read. What might have that survivor been thinking as they were experiencing their situation? What doubts might have they expressed? Try to step inside the shoes of "the survivor" and list the questions they might have asked themselves. Or list the questions you have about learning more about them and any other questions that you have about your reading.
>
> Now take those questions to create a poem. Consider mimicking Moore's style. Look for places to show knowledge about your topic and the lingering questions you'd like to have answered.

> My Sample Poem
>
> How did I get here?
> Is it always this cold?
> Where am I?
> It's too dark?
> Is this my friend's hand?
> Or a menacing creature I've never encountered?
> What's that sound?
> Is anyone else here?
> Can I really survive 42 days without eating?
> Is that my stomach growling?
> Mom?
> Where are you?
> I wish I'd listened to your warnings,
> oh, why didn't I?
> Did I already ask that question?

FIGURE 4.2 Twenty Questions writing prompt with sample poem by Barbara Edler.

As students wrote, I wandered the room, observing their drafting or answering questions. I noticed which students were on task and which students needed a little prompting to complete the assignment.

Mr. Muston wanted his students to complete the assignment the following day and later provided me with a folder of their typed poems; however, a few students could draft poems before the end of the period and invited me to read them. In other words, Lesson One can be a one or two-day lesson.

Several of the students' poems shared amazing feats of survival, from being trapped under a rock where a person was able to amputate their own arm to one plane crash survivor, to 9/

11 survivor events, and about people who survived war atrocities. Most students wrote their poems in a series of questions and some blended questions and answers.

Student Mia Fojtik's poem shared the story of Vulović, whose story is described in "13 People Who Survived the Unsurvivable." Vulović was the sole survivor of a plane crash that occurred over the Czech Republic. He received a Guinness World Record for surviving the most prolonged fall without a parachute. Mia's poem blends questions and provides thoughts her survivor might have had, demonstrating how students can empathize and establish a particular perspective through this creative writing approach.

Poem: Twenty Questions
What was that noise?
Was that an explosion?
Am I really falling this far down?
I wasn't supposed to work today.
I hope I don't die
Am I going to die?
What's happening?
This isn't real
I wanna go home
What happened to everyone else?
Am I really falling this far down?
How did the plane just explode?
Is everyone okay?
Should I check for others?
Am I the only one alive?
Are there others?
Am I going to survive this injury?

Ridley Delperdang wrote about a survivor of the Rwanda genocide, one of the topics, with a link shared in the presentation slides. In his notes, he identified that the survivor lost everyone she knew, was raped, and consequently contracted HIV.

I appreciated Ridley's ability to show the enormous trauma this survivor endured and how difficult this would be to articulate.

> Is this really happening?
> Why do they hate us so much?
> When can I get back to school?
> Who is going to save us?
> Why did he do that to me?
> Where is my family?
> Why my dad?
> Why my family?
> Why not me?
> Who could be that evil?
> Will I ever be normal again?
> Who is going to speak up for these people?
> Where are the women with their stories untold?
> Why can't things go back the way they were?
> How could anyone be so evil?
> How do I describe what happened to me?

Another student, Aria Maestro, wrote an emotional poem that illustrates a survivor's thoughts during the Itaewon Crush, which occurred at a Halloween festival on October 29, 2022 (Mackenzie, 2023). She begins her poem by describing her subject's experience, then adds questions to further identify the survivor's thoughts, and ends with the horror of the experience.

> Pressure.
> Pressure is all I felt.
> In my eyes
> In my ribs
> And in my chest.
> How did this happen?

How did I get here?
I don't understand.
Is anyone else feeling what I feel?
The pressure is growing.
I can't breathe.
Things fade from my vision.
The edges littered with polka-dots that replicated voids.
Just then,
Everything goes dark, and I can only hear the screams of others.

To summarize, students were beginning a unit of literature about surviving difficult situations, exploring ways humans overcome traumatic situations and the aftermath of a harrowing event, including experiencing survivor guilt. To begin the unit, students reviewed a list of possible topics provided on the slides. Students read online, took notes, and then wrote a poem using the twenty-question poetry prompt. Overall, the students showed their understanding and empathized with their survivors.

Although some students were not as engaged as others, most of them successfully showed their understanding of a survivor's story. One suggestion from a student was to provide more poetry prompts rather than just one. I had considered using a "found poem" format with them, and if I had to go back to do this again, I would demonstrate how to create a "paste pot" poem, which requires the writer to cull lines, phrases, and words from a text to create their poem. Having a variety of options is important. A "paste pot" poem takes longer but is a great exercise for tactile learners. Select words from the text, cut them out, and arrange/paste them onto another paper. The following poem is one I wrote about Ruby Bridges with words and lines taken from the previously mentioned McWhorter's text (Figure 4.3; p. 53).

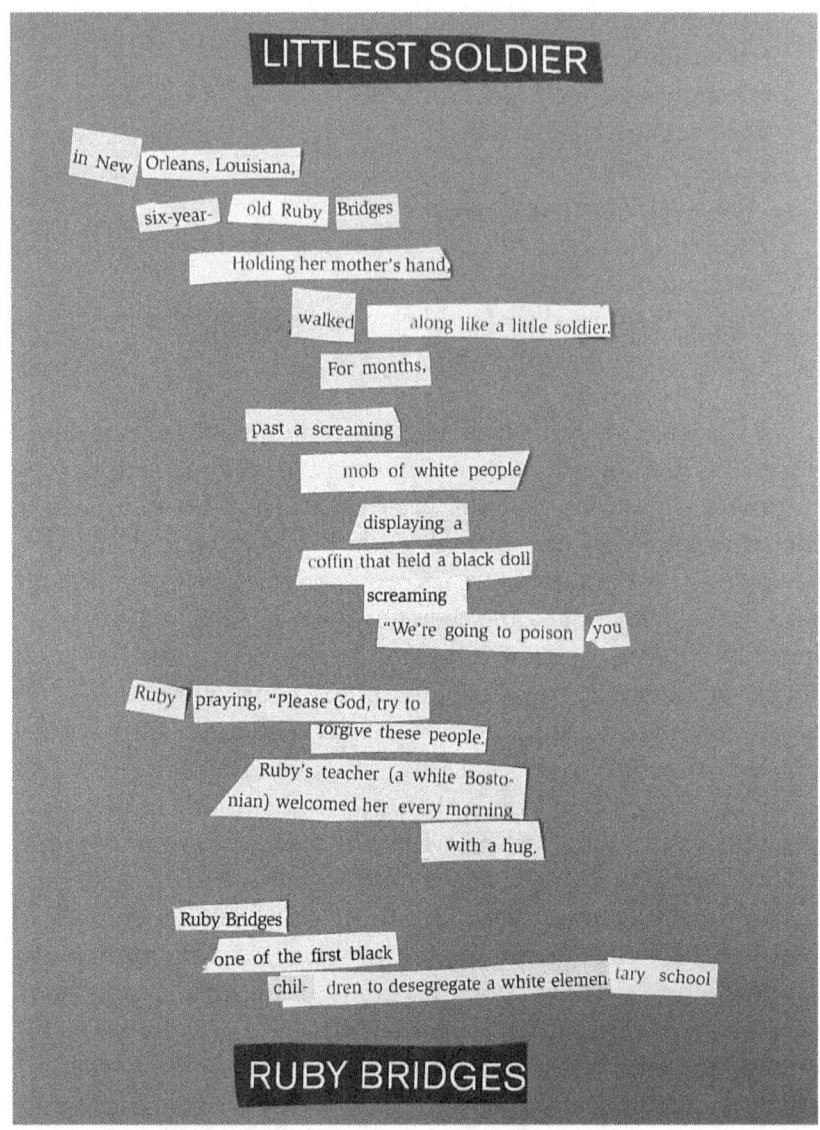

FIGURE 4.3 Image of a paste pot poem "Littlest Soldier" by Barbara Edler.

Sample Lesson: Science Biomolecules

Another class I visited was Mrs. Pfeiferling's Advanced Science class, a mix of first- and second-year high school students. Students were in the process of learning about biomolecules. Prior to meeting this class, I visited with Mrs. Pfeiferling to determine what she wanted the students to show about their learning. She wanted them to answer three questions about biomolecules: What are their unique characteristics? How do they function in the body? What foods would you find them in?

To begin this lesson, the students reviewed the critical questions on a Google slide (see Figure 4.4), which they could access from their online classroom. Students were encouraged to work in groups to answer the questions using notes they had previously taken in class or to refer to their textbook.

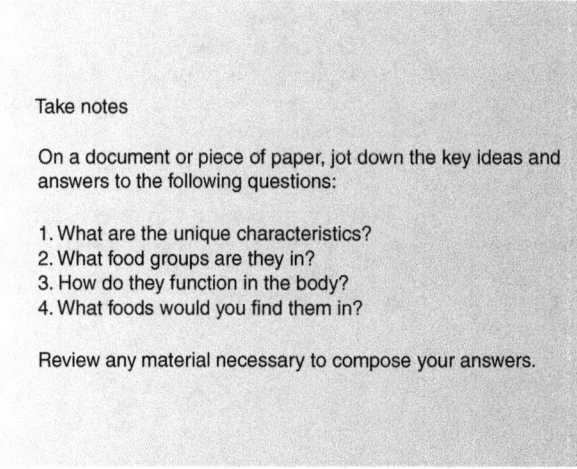

FIGURE 4.4 Presentation slide with note-taking directions.

For this class, I shared several ways for students to format a poem, which included acrostic, golden shovel, nonet, "piggyback poems," and diamante, with a link to creating this type of poem through an interactive tool provided at the *ReadWriteThink.org* website. Students were on task and collaborated well with each other. Mrs. Pfeiferling was also proactive in encouraging the students' progress and emphasizing that she wanted to see them complete all the tasks by the end of the period, which included answering the questions and drafting the poem.

In this session, students captured critical biomolecule facts through their poetry. Baylee Billing's poem focused on carbohydrates using the acrostic approach, which many students, I believe, find accessible for sharing their knowledge because they can define a term using its letters to format the poem. Baylee's poem could become a virtual notecard to study. Shown below are Baylee's notes that illustrate how she used and synthesized her recorded information to write about carbohydrates (Table 4.3).

TABLE 4.3 Students' Notes to Create an Acrostic Poem

Baylee's Carbohydrates Notes	
1. They are the body's first source of energy.	C – Carbon is present.
2. They are a biomolecule composed of Monosaccharides or simple sugars, such as Fructose and Glucose.	A – Animal's energy source.
	R – Ratio of two H atoms for one O atom by one C atom.
	B – Biomolecule.
	O – Oxygen is present.
3. They also have Disaccharides, which are two sugars and sucrose.	H – Hydrogen is present.
	Y – Your body needs them for survival.
4. And Polysaccharides, which are polymers.	D – Disaccharides.
	R – Perfect for living things.
a. Liver: glycogen, energy storage for animals.	A – Anyone can have them.
	T – They are helpful and can be tasty.
b. Potatoes: starch, the energy source for plants.	E – Energy source for plants and animals.
c. Cotton: cellulose supports the walls of plants and fiber for us.	S – Simple sugars.
5. Made of C – Carbon, H – Hydrogen, and O – Oxygen. The ratio of two H atoms to one O atom for every C atom.	

One student illustrated her knowledge of lipids by writing a diamante poem. The diamante form encourages the writer to not only define the selected term but also to make connections in the opening and closing lines as they choose a new term to define the topic. In the following student poem, we immediately know the topic is lipids because it is the poem's first word. The writer further develops the critical attributes of lipids, and in which foods it can be found. At the end of the poem, they make the connection that lipids are a form of energy.

Poem: Diamante
>Lipids
>Large biomolecules
>Carbon, Hydrogen, Oxygen
>olives, avocados, peanut butter, nuts, seeds, fish, dressing
>Part of the cell membrane
>Waxes, Fats, Oils
>Energy

Two other students used the acrostic format to show their understanding of proteins and nucleotides. Although acrostic poems would be lower on Bloom's taxonomy of knowledge, this type of writing is easily accessible to many students. More importantly, they are transferring their knowledge in a new way. By choosing this approach, writers can quickly formulate the key ideas of their topic. However, teachers could invite their students to dig deeper by analyzing their various poems. They could compare the poems, such as identifying the most important and the least important information. They could also look for any information they have left out and discuss if the missing pieces are vital to include. Diving into comparisons will further increase their depth of knowledge and level of engagement. (See Vanderbilt University for more information about Bloom's taxonomy).

Proteins
>Proteins help the body from muscle and bones.
>Really proteins are complex polymers.
>Oxygen, nitrogen, carbon, and hydrogen.
>Transport proteins to the cell membrane.
>Enzymes: speed up the rate of a chemical reaction without being used up in the reaction so that they can help many reactions occur.
>Inside of proteins are amino acids.
>Nuts, seeds, and soy products; all foods made from seafood; meat, poultry, and eggs; beans, peas, and lentils.

Nucleotides
    Universal to all forms of life
    Can't live without nucleic acid
    Life would not be possible
    Every living thing needs nucleic acid
    Impossible to survive without nucleic acids
    Complex molecule that stores cellular information in the form of a code

    All living things have nucleic acids
    Code
    In legumes, fish, mushrooms, meat, seafood, and all living things.
    DNA and RNA

In this class, students took advantage of collaborating with each other while using their previously taken notes. They then worked separately to write their poems, each focusing on a different biomolecule to further showcase their knowledge of all the molecules.

Sample Lesson - First Aid: CPR and AED

In Jessica Koehler's first aid class, students were at the end of CPR, cardiopulmonary resuscitation, and AED, which is an automated external defibrillator unit. During the previous class session, students had researched best practices for administering CPR and using an AED. My presentation for this class was similar to the one shared above about biomolecule lessons in the science class, where I shared several types of poem formats.

    I began the class with the following writing prompt: *Consider everything you know about CPR and AED. On a document or piece of paper, jot down the key ideas, steps, and reasons why knowing about these two things is essential. You will show your knowledge for this formative assessment assignment by writing a poem. Your poem doesn't have to be perfect or rhyme or have stanzas; it simply needs to illustrate to the reader what you know about CPR and AED creatively. The poem can be a free verse poem or follow a particular format.*

I then reviewed slides I created that shared various poetry formats, links to sample poems, and suggestions. (See Table 4.4). Students drafted their poems and then provided feedback to each other near the end of the period.

TABLE 4.4 Three Poetry Forms and Suggested Approaches to Writing a Poem Based on the Student's Knowledge

Nonet	A nonet is a nine-line poem with nine syllables in the first line, eight in the second line, and seven in the third line. It continues counting down until the final ninth line, which has one syllable. Samples of nonet poems can be found at poetrysoup.com.
Acrostic Poem	An acrostic poem is a form of poetry in which the first letters of each line represent a word, phrase, name, or short sentence when read vertically. The term displays the message or subject of the poem but does not need to rhyme or be formatted into stanzas. Consider writing your poem using one or both acronyms, CPR and AED.
Diamante Poem	Line 1: One-word topic (a noun) Line 2: Two adjectives Line 3: Three verbs Line 4: A four-word phrase Line 5: Three verbs Line 6: Two adjectives Line 7: A renaming noun for the topic A diamante interactive tool can be found at ReadWriteThink.org
Golden Shovel Poem	A Golden Shovel Poem is similar to the acrostic poem, but it asks the writer to borrow a line of poetry and to use each word from that line as the last word of each line in a new poem. For your prompt, take a sentence from your notes or copy one that captures the essence of CRP and AED. Now copy that sentence on the right side of the margin. Then, create a poem in which each line ends with the first to last word of that sentence.

Students drafted their poems in approximately 20 minutes. They wrote wonderful and insightful pieces about their topics, although several were unwilling to have their poems shared with a larger audience. Overall, they chose differing formats but clearly understood CPR and AED, and their poetry writing effectively encapsulated their overall knowledge. At this point, the students synthesized their knowledge and applied it in a different way.

The poetry writing allowed them to show the importance of life-saving skills and how and when these techniques would be applied.

Poem: Free Verse

The following student's free verse captured the process and an imagined event where CPR would be necessary.

> Hearts beat all around. Imagine
> If someone were to go down. You
> Panic and rush to their aid. Now
> Lay them down and pump pump pump. They
> May gasp for air, but do not jump. Check
> Their breathing in their chest. Though
> Don't go too hard, or you'll lay them to rest.

Although the writer uses some humor within the poem, the verse explains the necessary techniques to follow when using CPR.

In the next poem, Elizabeth Stambaugh's poetic response effectively illustrates how to perform CPR and why it is a critical skill to possess.

CPR

> Hands on the chest. Start the compressions,
> Rescue breaths, save them with compassion
> Heartbeat restored, a life saved

Elizabeth's succinct poem ends with the positive impact CPR can have. Her elbow partner also shared that she had clearly demonstrated her understanding of CPR.

Another student, Alexis Warth, combined both CPR and AED acronyms in her acrostic poem.

> **C**ompressions and consent
> **P**ractice makes perfect
> **R**eviving loved ones

Adult. Alive
Electric shock
Determined to save

Alexis' last line emphasizes the compassion these students were experiencing while learning about CPR and AED in their First Aid class.

After students drafted their poems, they completed a peer review. To structure their discussion, I asked them to listen carefully to each other and focus on what they found particularly striking in each other's poems. I also asked each writer to provide their own listening question for the reader/peer to respond to in order to share their own understanding of the poem.

Asking the students to peer review and comment on each other's poems allows them to hear each other's voices and articulate their understanding of the topic. Providing them with a structure while evaluating will also set parameters and a structure to aid their ability to respond.

As I listened to the students' peer reviews, I heard an elbow partner comment that she liked the writer's words and believed she understood CPR and AED better after reading her poem. Students could see how language could be manipulated to create a verse and show their knowledge. It was uplifting to hear them support each other's work and witness their feelings of success in creating something unique. Providing the time for students to read and respond to each other's poetry also allows them to review their shared knowledge and build a deeper understanding of the techniques and concepts.

In Alexis's poem, for example, she shows what she knows about CPR and identifies that administering CPR requires specific steps. I inferred from her poem that she understood the importance of practicing CPR to save someone suffering from a heart attack. Her second stanza is more figurative and brings a potential life-saving scene to life. Transferring her knowledge to an imagined crisis further reveals how she connected this information to a real-life situation and why it would be essential to retain this knowledge.

I asked all the students from each class to complete an exit slip to determine their engagement level, willingness to publish their poems, and the difficulty of the task they were asked to do. I also asked them for suggestions about the formative assessment. In the English class, where they were only given one type of poetry prompt, I read one suggestion that suggested providing more poetry approaches. I would follow this advice, but I cannot emphasize the importance of modeling.

Modeling our approach to the writing prompt will demonstrate to the students our willingness to take a risk with writing while providing a pathway to how they might compose the poem. For example, as students worked in the English classroom, several had difficulty beginning their poems. After showing them a few questions they might begin with, they had no trouble completing the writing. Writing with the students will further inspire them to see the value of showing their understanding of their topics through this creative writing approach.

Note: The following section provides adaptable guidelines that one can apply for writing poetry as a formative assessment. Each of these exercises provides a poetry prompt that could be used. Of course, a different poetry prompt could replace the suggested prompt, and each exercise can be adapted according to the learners' needs.

Three Poetic Exercises

Poetic Exercise One: Building Background Knowledge with Twenty Questions Poetry

Part One ~ Searching (15 to 20 minutes)
One of the first steps of research requires students to initiate an inquiry. In this lesson, students begin their research by attempting to locate a variety of quality resources. This first step will help students begin to hone in on what angle they want to present about a particular topic. Asking the students to generate a list of questions will help them explore the answers they seek. It will also provide them with direction and ownership of the research process.

This initial research step can be applied to any subject. For example, students might research a particular moment in history, a scientific study, or a person of interest. This could be focused on secondary sources one day and primary sources another, or students could look for secondary and primary information during their in-class search. Students could also dig into already prepared material to enhance their understanding of a particular issue, problem, event, etc., which could save time and potentially eliminate students from reading biased or flawed information.

Some students may need more support developing their questions. Consider using a graphic organizer with a variety of question types. For example, Sue Beers and Lou Howell's graphic organizer titled "Discussion Seeds" in the book *Reading Strategies in the Content Area, Vol. 2*, shares how to write different questions. By having students develop their questions, they are improving their metacognitive strategies, which according to Fisher, Frey, and Hattie's book *Visible Learning for Literacy*, self-verbalization, and self-questioning have a 0.64 percent impact on a student's learning (p.93).

Once the students have established which questions they want to explore, have them begin reading available journals and books provided or complete online searches. Sharing a list of website and journal links can make the time involved more productive and enable students to access quality information. After students have searched for 15 to 20 minutes, invite them to peruse their findings. Ask them to select their top two or three resources. Using highlighters or online tools, implore students to identify key concepts and ideas that will help answer their predetermined questions.

In Beers and Probst's book, *Reading Nonfiction: Notice and Note Stances, Signposts, and Strategies*, the authors found great success by having students note what surprised them. Through their studies, they identified four areas of surprise that engaged their students:

- New information ("I didn't know that");
- Suspicious information ("Really? Is that true?");
- Clarifying information ("Oh, Now I get it!";

- ♦ And a different perspective ("I hadn't thought of it that way") (p. 82). Providing students with an intentional structure will help them organize and retain the information they have reviewed. These notes will also provide a way for them to write their formative poem to showcase the knowledge they gained from their focused reading.

From these notations, challenge your students to write a poem to show their findings and current questions about their topic using Allison Berryhill's "Twenty Questions" poetry prompt from Ethical ELA's Open Write from February 15, 2020. This prompt will help students develop even more questions or the surprises they have discovered about their topic. Model your questions about a particular topic to help students see the benefits of developing a line of inquiry. By having students develop their series of questions, they will be able to take ownership and responsibility for their learning, two important ways to keep students engaged.

Part Two ~ The Poetry Prompt (10 minutes)

Allison Berryhill, an Iowa educator who teaches at Atlantic High School, shared Jim Moore's "Twenty Questions" with her 18-year-old son on the day he left for a year in New Zealand. The poem is ultimately about the choices we make in our lives and the lingering doubt that underpins those choices. Jim Moore's "Twenty Questions" poem is a series of self-reflective questions.

After reading Moore's poem on Poets.org, I invite you to write a question, then another, and follow it through memory and imagery until you have (maybe) twenty questions. Consider the choices that have made a difference in your life. Maybe end your poem with "Did I already ask that?"

For a research assignment, you may alter the latter part of this prompt by saying: *Consider the new information you have discovered today. Capture your questions about your topic and the questions you hope to answer as you continue your research until you have (maybe) twenty questions. The poem could also focus on a self-reflection that describes how much you, as a student, have learned about your topic through a series of questions.*

In the example below, Allison reflects on her classroom. Notice the inquiry: why, am I, where, why, will, what, and can?

"Twenty Questions From My Classroom" by Allison Berryhill

Why am I here?
In this chair, by this desk?
Am I flinging finite minutes of my life into the dusty swirl of students' too-full thoughts?
Are my words rolling tumbleweeds skirting across this barren plain?
Where is your hall pass?
Why am I wasting breath, breath, breath?
Will another Wednesday roll out from under me in 33-minute sprints?

What do they ask:
What did I miss yesterday?
Why are we reading this?
Where's Corbin Logeman?
And why do we say "have run" and not "have ran"?
Does it make a difference?
And to who?
Or to whom?
What is the color of teal?
Where is the receipt book?
Can I go to the nurse?

Do they learn anything?
Did I already ask that?

Part Three ~ Drafting: (15 to 20 minutes)
Have students draft their poems for 15 to 20 minutes.

You have your class routines, but we'd like to offer a few ideas here (that you will use in the other two lessons). First, we like **paper notebooks**. Paper notebooks are a clean break from technology and acquaint students with their natural handwritten font. They can also use the white space of the page and cross out. With digital notebooks, some of their ideas may be deleted, and you won't be able to witness the learning process. If students have notebooks open, you can easily walk around the room to see their progress. This is a live **assessment**. Of course, digital notebooks work, too, and some of your students may have accommodations requiring the use of technology, so do what is ethical and suitable for your students.

Modeling. We can't say enough about this part. You must start your poem in front of your students. Write the first few lines on the whiteboard or in your notebook that you project on your class screen with a document camera. Do a think-aloud about how you are coming up with the questions. What questions do you hear in your classroom? What are you wondering? All of these questions are starting points for research. If students are not used to writing regularly, they will need your help using the notebook, and their stamina may not be substantial. Be patient. The more you write with your students, the greater their stamina and joy. Note: You might want to try a sample poem before class if you are nervous about writing in front of students.

Live assessment. As noted above, it is the best time for assessment and feedback while students are writing. You can see their progress and quickly assess who needs your support. About three minutes into the writing, move around the room and watch. If students still need to get started, write with them. *How is it going? How can I help? Tell me what you are thinking. Let's write the first few lines together.*

The students are writing questions about a topic they are researching for you so that you can help them with your content knowledge expertise.

Part Four ~ Closing Self-Assessment: (5 to 10 minutes)
After the time is up, explain that their poem is a draft and begin having the students 1) pair/share their poems to begin the formative assessment or 2) complete the exit slip segment outlined below.

Assessment Options in Addition to the Poem:

1. Ask students to pair and share their poems. Then, have them work together to create inquiry questions to enhance their investigation. Their inquiry can be recorded in a research journal they create and use throughout their research project.
2. Ask students to complete an Exit Slip using the following format:

Record your thoughts ~

- 3 things you know about your topic
- 2 ways this topic connects to other topics
- 1 new question you have about this topic

<u>Alternative Prompt:</u>
Ask students to select key phrases and words from their readings. If possible, have them cut the words out. After they have compiled the words and phrases, invite them to arrange them on a piece of paper or construction paper to create a "found" poem or "paste pot" poem.

Poetic Exercise Two: Taking Notes, News, and New Poetry Prompt

Note-taking is a skill most teachers require students to practice because it helps students summarize critical ideas. Furthermore, note-taking can be one of the most effective learning skills a student can use throughout their lifetime. Using graphic organizers is a practical method for students to organize their notes and create nonlinguistic representations of their learning processes. Creating mental pictures of information is known to positively affect student achievement because it "stimulates and increases activity in the brain" (Marzano et al., 2001, p. 73). Any combination of note-taking can occur. Allowing students to choose a method will also help them recognize the power of recording information in a logical way that will not only deepen their understanding of what they are reading but also provide them easy access to the information they have found to be particularly important.

Part One ~ Note Taking: (15 to 20 minutes)

To begin this lesson, pre-select various graphic organizers for the students to adapt or use as they take notes. Take a minute or two to model your approach to organizing and recording notes. A few organization tools include the spider web, in which the topic is centered, and students record concrete facts on the web threads, which circle the topic. Another is an episode pattern organizer. This organizer uses the Episode at the top with the Cause to the left and the Effect to the right. Below the episode, students identify vital persons and record their notes below the various headings. A concept map, process/cause-effect pattern, or time sequence could also be modeled. One of my favorite graphic organizers is "Another Kind of Outline," which categorizes big ideas on the left and the details on the right (Table 4.5). As we saw in Baylee's note and poem, the details are used to craft her poem. (See Baylee's poem on Figure 4.1.)

TABLE 4.5 Big Ideas and Details About Organic Compounds

Big Ideas	Details
Organic compounds come from plants and animals	• water • carbon-containing molecules • made by living organisms • our bodies use them to maintain our body
Three common types of organic compounds	• carbohydrates • lipids • nucleic acids
Indicators change colors in the presence of a type of molecule	• dark red is positive for lipids • lighter pink is negative for lipids • blue-black is positive for starch (carb) • purple is positive for protein

Source: Adapted from Beers and Howell (2003). *Reading strategies for the content area, vol. 1* ASCD.

After students have decided how to record their notes, ask them to determine a purpose for their reading. For example, they might want to see which questions they can answer from the Pre-Search lesson, or you might ask them to look for author bias or "aha" moments. Establishing a purpose will guide students to read thoughtfully. Annotation marks can further provide students with ways to identify important passages and questions they have as they read. For example, a student may highlight a passage and place a large question mark in the margin along with a question they want to ask about the section. In another paragraph, they may add two exclamation marks to indicate a place that resonates for them or that they want to remember to include in their notes. Kylene Beers and Robert E. Probst's book *Note to Notice: Strategies for Close Reading* is an excellent source for instructors who want to find graphic organizers and strategies to support their students' ability to read literature and nonfiction closely.

Part Two ~ The Poetry Prompt: (10 minutes)

Whether you want your students to take notes throughout classes or during a set time frame, at the end of the note-taking session, invite students to write a poem that uses information from a text such as the one created by California educator Denise Krebs. Again, consider altering the text for this prompt to fit your purpose, but the main idea is to have the students dig into one or more of their sources to review the points that resonate with them.

Denise Krebs shared the following process to prime the writing: *Read articles that you resonate with, infuriate you, or you want to spend more time with and make sense of the content through poetry. Choose one article and read it with a notebook and pencil in hand. Write down all the phrases and words that jump out at you. Turn these into a poem, along with your own words. Try a free verse poem, as I did, or a poetic form that gives you more of a challenge if you wish. Share the source article when you post your poem.*

Denise, an active Ethical ELA writer, had been reading about George Floyd's and Ahmaud Arbery's deaths to gain a better awareness of the injustices Black people who live in the United States face. Adam Sewer's article from the *Atlantic*, titled "The Coronavirus Was an Emergency Until Trump Found Out Who Was Dying" focuses on racial discrimination and how some lives during the pandemic were viewed as more worthy than others. Denise said that sometimes, she highlighted lines but changed the form a bit and marked where these changed quotes occurred. For instance, "two armed white men had a right to self-defense" became *"Two armed white men* insist on their *right to defend themselves"* and "the racial contract most often operates unnoticed, relying on Americans to have an implicit understanding of who is bound by the rules, and who is exempt from them." In her poem, this became *Americans implicitly know/Who are bound by the rules/*And *who are exempt.* Many words and phrases were selected from the first half of this article where Serwer describes the racial contract in America. She used italics to demonstrate which words she borrowed from the text. Students could follow Denise's process to identify when they use the author's language in their own found poem.

"Say His Name—Ahmaud Arbery" by Denise Krebs

"Come, son, grab your gun.
There's a black burglar.
Bounding 'round the block"

In this land
Two armed white men insist on their
right to defend themselves
While one unarmed black man
is *not allowed to exercise the same right*
Or to exercise

State laws made to justify
Two people
Chasing,
Confronting, and
Killing
a person
they've never met.
Usurping duties of
police, court, jury,
and executioner.

As long as the two
are on the safe side
of the racial contract in 'Merica
they will be exonerated.
Always
Assumptions of white innocence
Always
Assumptions of black guilt
Always

Americans implicitly know
Who are bound by the rules
And *who are exempt*
Would your son be allowed to jog
in a new neighborhood?
I know
You know

All men are created equal
(If they are white and own property)
Crooked creed

All men are created equal
(But some are only three-fifths equal)
Crippling creed

Codicil in invisible ink
Yet penned visibly in red blood
On black bodies

Murder is illegal
But fine for white people to
Chase down and kill black people
If they have decided
That those black people scare them
Cowardly creed

These injustices
Push the racial contract into the open
Then it's up to us to choose
Do we *embrace its existence?*
Do we *contest* its existence?
Do we *deny* its existence?

Hang on, white men.
Hang on, power-hungry,
To your fading entrenchment of
White political power to
"make America great again"

Father and son
Chased a "burglar" jogger
Shot him dead.
Acting in self-defense?
No.
Arrested and charged with murder
Because of *national outrage*
(But absent the video, then what?)

Centuries overdue,
But now is the time
for more
national outrage,
America.
It's time for a
Courageous creed

How would you, the teacher, assess Denise's understanding of the article? Notice how she italicized some of the words to show where she pulled words directly from the text and her evolving perspective on the issue. Imagine your students writing a poem from one or more of their compiled resources. Students could be asked to consider how the author's tone and perspective impact the content, and the readers/students could also show their own stance on the issue or topic.

Part Three ~ Drafting: (15 to 20 minutes)
Have students draft their poems for 15 to 20 minutes using words and information they pulled from one or more articles. **Please refer back to Lesson One: Drafting for more details on how to facilitate this part.**

Part Four ~ Closing Self-assessment: (5 to 10 minutes)
Have students participate in a Socratic Seminar using open-ended questions to lead a discussion (See *Socratic Questions: Center for Excellence in Teaching and Learning*, uconn.edu). As the discussion unfolds, participants listen closely, responding to others, encouraging each other through follow-up questions, and piggybacking off what others have said. This technique is especially effective when you have students review the key expectations of a discussion as follows:

- Speaks in the discussion
- Makes eye contact with other speakers or as she/he/they speak
- Refers to the text
- Ask a new or follow-up question
- Responds to another speaker
- Paraphrases and adds to another speaker's ideas
- Encourages another participant to speak

For this activity/discussion, have each student share their poem and develop a question they will ask their listeners to answer about their poem. For example, the student might ask one of the following questions:

1. What did you learn from my poem?
2. How did my poem expand your understanding of my topic?
3. What questions do you have about my subject that I should answer?
4. Which part is the most vivid?
5. Which part is the most unclear?

You can also set a time limit depending on how you arrange the Socratic Seminars. For example, if you have groups of five, it may take 30 minutes to complete the discussion. Each person in the group could have 5 to 7 minutes to share and have their poem discussed. Again, you can adjust the group size and time limit to suit your class period.

Poetic Exercise Three: The Final Product & Capturing Voices from the Past

This lesson is for after students have completed their research. This may mean students have read multiple sources and written multiple poems. You may have students submit a portfolio of their notes and poems to demonstrate their learning. A research paper variation called The Multigenre Project shows how to help students organize their poetry by using reading notes and a letter to the reader sharing the research process. Read more on Colorado State University's website, "Introduction to Multigenre." This lesson offers a way for students to create a summative project by writing a poem that they then share with peers so that students can learn from one another. What is great about writing poetry, again, is that students can read multiple poems in one class period. Typical research papers are too long for teachers to read, let alone a class of high school students in a 50-minute class period.

Part One ~ Final Reflection: (5 minutes)

Once students have completed researching their particular topic, such as a personal search about their birth year, a scientific discovery, how a war impacted society, the techniques an artist uses to establish a mood, or the best techniques for saving money and buying a car, ask them to write creatively to demonstrate their knowledge. Of course, not all research or paths of inquiry need to generate a summative project, but if students have invested a lot of class time studying a subject, it makes sense to have a final artifact to share their learning with an authentic audience.

For this final lesson, you could have students assess what they have learned in various ways. For example, consider the following options:

- Have students consider the voices they have encountered in their research and create a poem that will formatively assess what they learned from these varied voices as they read.
- Have students write a poem that demonstrates the knowledge they have gained and provides a deeper insight into what they have learned.
- Have students consider what they think it would have been like for them during that time period. This can help them show empathy and understanding, such as with a unit focused on the Civil Rights Movement, which is not only complex and multifaceted but also rich with a variety of outstanding and compelling leaders and witnesses.
- Have students focus on a commanding or engaging tone as they read.
- Have students identify which source was their best source of information because of its currency, relevance, authority, accuracy, and purpose.
- Have students identify the biases they encountered or perhaps even conflicting information.
- Lastly, students should demonstrate what they have learned by writing poems to show their knowledge.
- Have students reflect on what they learned about their writing process or how they used language in poetry to express their newfound discoveries.

The door is wide open. Choose which option works best for your teaching goals, but remember the power of self-assessment. This is an opportunity for students to articulate how far they have come. As a final assessment to be graded, consider having the students create a collection of their poems, such as the multigenre project noted above or a portfolio. Many websites show teachers how to facilitate a portfolio presentation, but students love Canva and slides to format their poems with images and new fonts.

If students choose to revise, they could also write a reflection about what they learned throughout their research, how they used poetry to show their knowledge, and what changes they made afterward to clarify their messages.

Part Two ~ The Poetry Prompt: (10 minutes)
Oklahoma teacher educator Sarah Donovan inspired writers to capture voices from the past. Her post 23 #Verselove with Kip Wilson is compelling and a perfect prompt to close a focused research activity. Sarah said, "Inspiring figures from the past can just as easily inspire us today. Poetry provides the perfect medium for capturing voices from the past." I have seen more and more teachers reaching across the ELA and Social Studies curricula for lessons that fall under both umbrellas, and this is a great exercise and way to experiment with both.

If you have a historical figure who has long fascinated you, take a moment from their life and imagine what they might have been thinking or feeling. While this is probably easiest using a well-known figure with plentiful information available, even a quick Google search can yield enough basic information to create a snapshot."

"Marta Husemann, 1937" by Kip Wilson

After acting for
Bertolt Brecht in
Kuhle Wampe

and for
my own sake under
Gestapo interrogation

once
twice

before being sent
to Moringen Concentration Camp
in 1937

I know I will have to perform.
like I never have
before when I walk out of
here and into the

undercover
life
I'm even more
determined to lead now.

Part Three ~ Drafting: (15 to 20 minutes)

Have students draft their poems for 15 to 20 minutes. Allow them to review the other two poems and the notes that they have taken. To further help students compose their poems, share specific poetry formats such as Etheree, Cinquain, or Triolet. (Refer to Table 4.6 chart with suggested poetic formats.) Poetryfoundation.org has several resources to assist students in understanding poetic forms and mentor poems they could model for their poems. I highly recommend modeling to your students how to mimic the poet's style by choosing new words for the poetry lines and placing the new words in a similar arrangement to the original poet's poem, often called a "Piggyback" poem.

TABLE 4.6 Poem Form Variations

Tanka: A tanka is one of the oldest Japanese poetry forms. It has five lines that follow a specific pattern: Line one has five syllables, Line two has seven syllables, Line three has five syllables, and Lines six and seven have seven syllables.	**Triolet:** A triolet is an eight-line poem that uses only two rhymes throughout: ABaAabAB.
Etheree: An etheree is similar to a nonet, except it is a ten-line poem in which the first line begins with one syllable, the second line with two syllables, and the final line has ten syllables.	**Palindrome:** A poem that reads the same forward or backward. It is a mirror poem.
Cinquain: Cinquains are short, structured poems. They are five lines long. The first line has two syllables; the second has four syllables; the third has six syllables; the fourth has eight syllables and two syllables in the last line. Most cinquains will have a connecting idea or synonym for the first and last lines.	**Ekphrasis:** An ekphrastic poem is a descriptive response to a piece of art, real or imagined. Generally, the writer will expand on the meaning of the subject.
Concrete Poem: A concrete poem uses words to shape the subject. It is a perfect poetic form for students who want to visualize the subject.	**Ballad:** A narrative poem that generally follows the rhyme scheme ABCB and is organized into quatrains.

Part Four ~ Closing Self-Assessment: (5 to 10 minutes)
Ask the students to participate in a "Gallery Walk," which creates a classroom museum where students will review posted material, often providing commentary on sticky notes that they place near or on the displayed document. Gallery Walks are one of my favorite activities because it encourages movement. To prepare students for a Gallery Walk, be sure to set up clear expectations for purposeful engagement. Remind them not to use language that could be conveyed as harmful. Again, modeling this activity with your students will further its success. The following source can further help you plan a gallery walk: Gallery-Walk.pdf (harvard.edu)

To begin the Gallery Walk, ask students to display their poems around the room. The poems could be placed on a larger piece of white paper with Post-it notes available for peers to record their thoughts about what they learned from each poem. A smaller gallery walk could take place by dividing the room into sections and having each small group view their "corner" of the room, etc.

For this gallery walk, demonstrate how to write specific commentary using sentence starters such as the following. Students can write these on sticky notes and stick them beside the poem. At the end, students can collect their poems and celebratory sticky notes:

- *The one thing I learned from this poem is*
- *One image that stood out to me while reading the poem was*
- *I could hear*
- *I could see*
- *This poem makes me question*
- *Your poem is inspiring because*

Other Closing Assessment Options:

1. Have students record their poetry and post the recordings online. Padlet.com is a free online tool where students can record themselves reading their poetry or create an

audio recording of their work. Students can respond with ratings and comments.
2. Have students create a portfolio with poems, drafts, self-assessments, notes, and other nonlinguistic representations of their learning process.
3. Have students individually or collaboratively create a multi-genre piece to be shared in small or large groups. Consider publishing their work on a school website.

While each prompt provides a particular way to respond, you may also want to share alternative poetry formats with the students. Refer to the poetry chart and website to share potential poetry forms.

Conclusion

Please consider using these poetry prompts and strategies to assess your students' inquiry pursuits formatively. Writing poetry will provide an engaging way for students to exhibit their knowledge. Discussing the poetry will further enhance their connections and understanding of any topic. Writing poetry as a formative assessment allows you to evaluate students' understanding and struggles quickly. It is a win/win situation for both you and your students. Years of my own personal teaching experience have proven that discussions about poetry often lead students to a deeper understanding of topics far more meaningful than typical worksheets or question-and-answer routines because it personalizes their learning and allows them to express themselves. More importantly, poetry provides the ultimate learning ladder because it meets students where they are on their knowledge of a topic and urges them to climb—which is at the heart of lifelong learning!

References

Andrews, E. (2024, March 12). *10 things you should know about the Donner Party*. HISTORY. www.history.com/news/10-things-you-should-know-about-the-donner-party.

Beers, K. & Probst, R. (2013). *Notice & note: strategies for close reading.* Heinemann.

Beers, S. & Howell, L. (2003). *Reading strategies for the content area, vol. 1.* ASCD.

Beers, S. & Howell, L. (2005). *Reading strategies for the content area, vol. 2.* ASCD.

Berryhill, A. (2020). "Twenty questions from my classroom." February, day 1/5 twenty question poems. *Ethical ELA.* February, Day 1/5: Twenty Questions Poems – Ethical ELA.

Fisher, D., Fry, N. & Hattie, J. (2016). *Visible learning for literacy.* Corwin Literacy.

Krebs, D. (2020). September # open write: News and new. Ethical ELA. September's #OpenWrite: News and New – Ethical ELA.

Langstraat, L. (n.d.). Multigenre: An introduction. *Writing: Colostate.* https://writing.colostate.edu/gallery/multigenre/introduction.htm.

London, J. (1908). *To build a fire.* The Century Magazine.

Mackenzie, J. (25 October 2023). Itaewon crush: survivors are still tormented a year on. *BBC News.* www.bbc.com/news/67203564.

Marzano, R., Pickering, D. & Pollock, J. (2001). *Classroom instruction that works.* ASCD.

McHorter, D. (2004). *A dream of freedom: The civil rights movement from 1954 to 1968.* Scholastic Nonfiction.

Mehrotra, A. (2015, June 17). *20 last known survivors of major historic events.* ScoopWhoop. www.scoopwhoop.com/world/last-survivors-historic-events/.

Moore, J. (2012). Twenty questions. Twenty Questions by Jim Moore – Poems. Academy of American Poets. https://poets.org/poem/twenty-questions

Opalschool.org (2019). *Gallery walk.* Gallery-Walk.pdf (harvard.edu).

PoetrySoup. (n.d.). *Nonet poems.* PoetrySoup. www.poetrysoup.com/poems/nonet#google_vignette.

ReadWriteThink. (n.d.). *Diamante poems.* National Council of Teachers of English. www.readwritethink.org/classroom-resources/student-interactives/diamante-poems.

Serwer, A. (2020, May 8). The coronavirus was an emergency until Trump found out who was dying. *The Atlantic.*

University of Connecticut. (n.d.). Socratic questions. https://cetl.uconn.edu/resources/teaching-your-course/leading-effective-discussions/socratic-questions/.

Vanderbilt University Center for Teaching. (n.d.). *Bloom's taxonomy*. Vanderbilt University. https://cft.vanderbilt.edu/guides-sub-pages/blooms-taxonomy/

Wilson, K. (2019). Marta Husemann, 1937. 23 #verselove2019 with Kip Wilson. *Ethical ElA*. 23 #verselove2019 with Kip Wilson – Ethical ELA. https://ethicalela.com/23-verselove2019-with-kip-wilson/

5

Unlocking Language Poetry as a Tool for Vocabulary Study

Gayle Sands

The Importance of Vocabulary Comprehension (and How Poetry Can Help)

If our students don't know what the words in the text mean, they aren't going to understand the content. This is a "no-duh" statement that is easy to agree with. The problem is, sometimes, our students aren't aware that they *don't* know the meaning of critically essential vocabulary words. Often, students read to get to the end of the page, to be done with it. In their race to the finish, they forget that they are supposed to *comprehend* the text (Vacca & Vacca, 2002). In the students' minds, if they have decoded the words, they have completed the assignment. We all know that's not the case. Decoding does not equal understanding.

I taught middle-school English/Language Arts for 27 years. Although I had students of all ability levels, I had a proclivity for students who needed extra support. In my five years as a reading resource teacher, I "pushed in" to science and social studies classes to assist new teachers with lesson planning, presentation, and classroom management. I now work as an adjunct for a local college, supervising and advising education practicum students in all subjects and grade levels. My experience has shown me, again and again, that vocabulary comprehension is vital to our students' ability to process what they read, no matter what subject we are talking about.

It is easy to fall back on the ever-popular "copy, define, and use in a sentence" method to introduce and review academic and curriculum-specific vocabulary. That strategy is enough for some students, but many learners need more.

A variety of views exist about when and how to teach vocabulary (Marzano, 2004; Roe, Smith &, Burns, 2011; Vacca & Vacca, 2002). Some teachers assign a list of vocabulary words on Monday; during the week, students memorize them or take notes. Later in the week or at the end of the unit, the words appear in a test section where they match terms with definitions. Memorizing lists is one version of pre-teaching (Vacca & Vacca, 2002), but we can do better. I like to approach vocabulary lists as inviting word *study* rather than *memorization*. We want students to study the words in various ways—in isolation to recognize word parts (e.g., non, anti, pheno, geno), in context for specific meanings, and connection to their lives.

Words essential to subject mastery in a particular unit can be introduced before reading or lectures, emphasized during reading and practice, and/or reviewed afterward (ideally in a new context) to improve and assess readers' understanding and comprehension (Vacca & Vacca, 2002).

Poetry can productively enter any of these stages—to introduce vocabulary, play with vocabulary, and assess vocabulary understanding. Writing poetry is especially valuable as a post-reading/unit review of essential terms. It works well as a formative assessment to evaluate student readiness to tackle an exam or another summative assessment.

Poetry can support vocabulary acquisition to engage students' interest and bolster comprehension. In *Reading to Learn in the Content Areas,* Richardson, Morgan, and Fleener state, "Creating an environment for encouraging language play, inquiry, and discovery in addition to planning explicit instruction provides a means for positively influencing vocabulary acquisition to include both intentional and incidental learning pathways" (2009, p. 175). Play. Inquiry. Discovery. All of these are inherent in poetry. When you invite students to write poetry infused with their vocabulary words, their word study becomes intentional and relevant.

I know from visiting many content-area classes that poetry is a pathway that is only sometimes considered for non-English/Literature classes. However, it is a pathway worth implementing. In *Reading to Learn in the Content Areas* (2009), Richardson, Morgan, and Fleener state, "Poetry, like science, mathematics, social studies, and other content areas, involves reasoning, understanding, and making connections to the world. At the same time, it provides a means for appreciating the power and subtleties found and expressed through words" (p. 235). I hope this chapter persuades you that poetry can work in *your* classroom.

Poetry Outside of English Class

But…Poetry in Math? Social Studies? Science? Art? *In MY class?*

Cue the protest: Poetry? In MY class? But I teach History (or Math, Science, Spanish—you fill in the blank). Poetry belongs in English class. All that rhyme scheme, looking for the hidden message, blah, blah, blah stuff. I left that behind a long time ago!

I get it—you have enough on your plate just to get the curriculum out there. Before you close the chapter, let me present my case. Poetry does not have to rhyme and does not insist that you analyze metaphors, similes, or any literature-specific terminology you ran away from. Think of poetry writing as defining and playing with words to *build meaning*—and deep meaning is the goal of vocabulary mastery.

Bridges to Literature (2002) provides this simple definition of poetry: "Poetry is literature that uses a few words to tell about ideas, feelings, and images" (p. 463). I like William Carlo Williams' (1944) definition better. In his essay "Introduction to the Wedge," he states that "a poem is a small (or large) machine made of words" (pp 256–257). We can build students' vocabulary through the machine of poetry.

Poetry writing provides the opportunity to have fun with words while reinforcing the vocabulary our students need. I have always viewed poetry as a clarification of ideas, a distillation of concepts. We offer important concepts in a minimum of words. Isn't that what vocabulary is—distilled information? Assigning students to create poems provides a way to step back from flashcard drills, matching, and definition dumps and infuse higher-order thinking into the learning process.

Developing assignments to write poems offers a meaningful strategy to help your students build content *and* context knowledge. In *Bringing Words to Life: Robust Vocabulary Instruction* (2002), I. Beck, M. McKeown, and L. Kucan (2002) discuss that building a deeper understanding of one word or concept enhances the grasp of other words or ideas related to meaning. By broadening a student's knowledge of one term, you enrich their comprehension of related terms and ideas. Learning doesn't occur in a vacuum; one word at a time. It connects one idea to another and then another. Learners who explore subject-specific vocabulary words innovatively expand their understanding and comprehension.

Two Poetic Forms: The Sevenling & Hay(na)ku

This chapter provides lessons and examples for two poem *forms*—the Sevenling, a simple seven-line poem, and the Hay(na)ku, an offshoot of the haiku (that 5-7-5 poem that had you counting syllables on your fingers). Relax—I am not going to bombard you with literature terminology (I can't resist giving you a tiny bit, though…).

The term poetic *form* means the poem's structure—the arrangement of the words or what they will look like on the page. Some poems have *stanzas,* a way of grouping lines and building meaning. The forms in this chapter encourage students to focus on the meaning of their vocabulary words beyond just the dictionary/text definition. It pushes them to dig deeper into concepts/vocabulary terms. They build connections between the textbook definition and how the word operates in the "real world"—in their world. These connections create multiple avenues for grasping the concepts in a text. An introduction to the two forms will help you see where we are going with this.

Poets organize lines in a poem to move toward some sort of discovery of their topic. The **Sevenling** was presented by British poet Roddy Lumsden (Lumsden, 2004). It is a seven-line poem (no surprise). In the Science Sevenling, I wrote as a model, "Diffusion;" I began with the technical definition of diffusion found on the website CK12.org: "The process by which molecules move from an area of higher concentration to an area of lower concentration." I considered my experiences with "molecules" moving from higher to lower concentrations. Of course, I thought of school.

The first stanza of this Sevenling invites us to picture students and teachers leaving at the end of the school year and going their separate ways (diffusing). The second stanza addresses the opposite or contrast to diffusion—a coming together of students and teachers as they return in the fall. The final line of the sevenling gets us deeper into the concept of diffusion as a nod to how education is managed. In many states, students don't have a choice to exit voluntarily until they are 16. Based on that rule, those students can't reverse the diffusion process (to "de-diffuse" a made-up word) at will. Using this concept encourages students to think about other examples of diffusion (Table 5.1).

TABLE 5.1 Two-Column Example of Sevenling; Format on Left Column and Model "Diffusion" on Right by Gayle Sands

Sevenling: a seven-line poem–consisting of two 3-line stanzas and a single final line.	**Model: Science Sevenling**
	"Diffusion" by Gayle Sands
Stanza 1: 3 lines: What the vocabulary word means, an example	On the last day of school before summer-- we *diffuse* from the school We scatter, we spread out, we splatter our smiles on the world. Life is good. *Diffusion*!
Stanza 2: 3 lines: a contrast--can be opposite or just different	But remember, school awaits us. We will reassemble, congregate, and concentrate…. *Diffusion* cannot last forever
Closing: 1 line: something to think about, another connection.	We cannot refuse to "de-diffuse."

A Hay(na)ku is a 3-line poem. This form, derived from the traditional haiku, was invented in 2003 by Filipino poet Eileen Tabios (Tabios, 2005). It consists of one word in the first line, two in the second line, and three in the third line. You can stop there, but for a deeper meaning of the vocabulary word, you can make it a Reverse Hay(na)ku (Tabios, 2005) by adding a second stanza (three words, two words, one word) to chain together the short form into something longer. We like two stanzas so students can write more and see how the concept works in reverse. Unlike Haiku, the focus is on *words* and not syllables. In my example below, you can see that I moved into a history class and used the historical term "Daoism" (Laozi, 1988), a Chinese belief focused on harmony with nature's way and maintaining balance in everything. For this poem, I would ask students to brainstorm their version of nature and where they feel in harmony. The harmony of nature could be outdoors, but it could also be their bedroom or basketball court. Where do they feel in harmony—both in their physical body and their psychological space?

For me, harmony is attained when I sit in my backyard listening to an audiobook and working on my latest watercolor project. Before you begin, consider what your version of harmony might be. Students will learn the historical context of this term in your class. However, the sense of harmony, the sense of physical and psychological balance, is part of understanding the concept of Daoism. Writing poetry illuminates the term. The connections show them why learning more about the topic and their broader understanding of the world might be relevant to them (Table 5.2).

TABLE 5.2 Two-Column Chart With the Format of Hay(na)ku on the Left and Model Poem on the Right by Gayle Sands

Hay(na)ku	Social Studies Hay(na)ku
	"Daoism" by Gayle Sands
• Line 1: 1 word	Simple
• Line 2: 2 words	Nature's way
• Line 3: 3 words	Yin and Yang
(reverse it!)	
• Line 4: 3 words	Shaded and sunlit
• Line 5: 2 words	Balance opposites
• Line 6: 1 word	Acceptance

The Lesson Plan: Six Tasks

The primary lesson plan is the same for both forms and can be adapted to any form and any subject area—you'll see. Trust me. Once you have become comfortable with the poetic forms provided here, other forms can easily be swapped in using the same essential lesson organization. An online search offers a wealth of alternate poetic forms if you choose to branch out for future lessons. This website, *Learn About Poetry, Different Types of Poems, and Poetic Devices With Examples—2024— MasterClass*, discusses some of the more common forms with examples and without a surplus of literary jargon. You can also use forms from the other chapters to study vocabulary.

I taught both forms—Sevenlings (with model poems for diffusion, mitosis, and genetics) and Hay(na)kus (with models for recessive genes and phenotypes) to two 7th-grade science classes in my hometown in rural Maryland. I wanted to be sure the lesson plan was foolproof—or as foolproof as any lesson can be with seventh graders. Each of the classes I worked with had a mix of 25 on-level and above-average students preparing for their final test on a genetics unit. Their science teacher, a long-time friend, was game to try a new review process for the vocabulary portion of the exam. She had already taught the unit, so the students were familiar with the terms, although it was obvious that they had forgotten some of them when we did a quick review before writing.

The students were high-energy and talkative. After they completed the lesson, I asked them for feedback. Most expressed enthusiasm about the lesson. I incorporated their suggestions about improvements I could make into the lesson you see below. I will share some of their poems following the lesson plan.

The Lesson Plan—at Last!

If you are a Social Studies, Math, or World Language teacher, please consider the unit you are teaching/planning now and the key terms you might use. The Basic Lesson Plan has six tasks and takes two days. I did the actual teaching in one 75-minute class period.

If you want to view the entire process before we begin, go to the **Basic Lesson Plan, Table 5.9**, at the end of this chapter. In the left column, I have listed what you should do to prepare for the lesson. In the right column, I have examples from my science lesson.

The Tasks: An Introduction

Task 1: Choose the words.
Task 2: Divide the list/assign the words
Task 3: Introduce the Poetic Forms
Task 4: Introduce the Inquiry Process
Task 5: Provide graphic organizers and rubrics
Task 6: Share the Knowledge

Task 1: Term Selection

Select the terms before you begin planning the lesson. First, determine the essential vocabulary words you want your students to study. When I taught the science class, we were focusing on the role of the Punnett Square as a predictor of the results of genetic crosses, so we selected the following words: probability, Punnett Square, phenotype, genotype, dominant, recessive, codominance, and gene. Remember to think of a specific lesson in *your* unit as you read this proposal.

On the first day of the activity, as in typical vocabulary lessons, you will hand out the definitions on paper or digitally. If you are using the plan to introduce new vocabulary, students should enter them (digitally or physically) into their notebooks for easy reference. Then, do a mini-lecture or show graphics to provide the context of vocabulary's context. This background is necessary before beginning to write and could be done in one class period.

Because my lesson was a review, I provided an online list with definitions for students to access on their Chromebooks. The students were already familiar with the terms, so I did a quick run-through to ensure everyone was comfortable. Students referred to their notes in their notebooks during the discussion. It took about 15 minutes to complete the review before we began writing.

Caution: If any words lend themselves to off-color interpretations, you have a couple of choices. You can delete the words from the list or address the issue of inappropriate meanings upfront to make it clear that they will not be accepted. I taught middle school and have regrettable memories of the students enjoying alternate off-color meanings of any vocabulary terms when given the opportunity.

A few pro tips:

1. Be sure to complete the introduction and review of the vocabulary terms before students begin writing their poems. Even if they tell you they know the words, some are probably recognized, not remembered.
2. Consideration: Additional support may be necessary for words not easily defined using textbook definitions. In

this case, provide images, videos, or other text to provide the context needed for student inquiry.
3. This lesson is especially practical as a post-reading, pretest review, and formative assessment after you have gone through the text. Students will have already built a context for the terms, and their poetry will reflect that.

Task 2: Divide/Assign Words to Groups or Individuals

Students have notes on key conceptual words of your unit. They have the list. They have some of your lecture notes. But these words may have little meaning—yet. Students need to study the words. We can make connections that will clock in on the concepts by offering the opportunity to play with the words as they learn them.

For this part, you must consider the makeup of your class and the grouping that works best for them. (Doubet, 2022; Silberman, 2006). Word study works well when students can talk things through. Being with other learners with different learning experiences helps correct misunderstandings and offer broader perspectives.

Decide whether the groups will consist of student pairs, groups, or students working individually (Herrera et al., 2011). You know your class—decide how you want them to interact. I have found that a group larger than three results in more socialization than productive writing. If a student wants to work alone, I generally let them do so, but then check in with them to offer a chance to discuss what they are doing.

This lesson is all about writing a poem around a single word. Your present task is to assign terms. Depending on your class size, you may need to assign each term to more than one group. That is okay; seeing how the poems vary using the same vocabulary term will be surprising. Here are a few ways to approach it:

1. You assign them. No student choice.
2. Use popsicle sticks, grab bags, and playing cards to determine the selection order.
3. Use an online randomizer to assign words OR to determine the chosen order. A free online source is *Wheel of Names*.

In my trial run with the 7th graders, I let them choose groups of no more than three. I allowed each group to pick whatever word they wanted to write about. As a result, I saw that some words were not used, and some were done in more than one group. I learned from my mistake, and I recommend you use one of the options offered above to ensure that all terms are addressed.

Task 3: Introduce the Poetic Forms

We have reached the part you might have dreaded—writing the *poetry*.

You have accomplished a lot. You have selected words, offered standard definitions and some context, and carved time for inquiry. Now, students will synthesize their research and thinking into a poem so you can assess their understanding.

You have likely been assessing all along. Did you note what they were researching, how they used the thesaurus, and the conversations with other students? Did you stop the flow of learning to clarify something? If so, you assessed and were responsive as they learned. Teachers constantly assess without even thinking about it. It happens so naturally that we forget to give ourselves credit for it,

You are about to introduce the lesson. Discuss why you use poetry to help them review their vocabulary terms. Let us start with the Sevenling. I have provided a script for reference. The script is not prescriptive—just an example.

Sample Science Lesson Script

In an ideal world, lesson plans make sense the first time you read them. My world has never proven ideal, and I have wasted too much time interpreting another person's planning. Here, I will attempt to provide enough supporting material to save you the time wasted on confusion. I presented the lesson via PowerPoint (Figure 5.1). All of the slides I used are included below. Of course, the slides, charts, visuals, and model script are not prescriptive—use, change, or replace them. I am sure you will add images to yours. These are the bare bones of my lesson. It is your classroom and your vocabulary list—do what you will!

Here we go…

Gayle: Today, you will write a poem to help you remember your vocabulary words for the test on Friday. I know this seems strange--you are not in English class--but it will work! (Have someone read the Objectives and Explanation)

Objectives

- Students will review/learn new vocabulary terms and apply them using two poetic forms: the **Sevenling** and the **Hay(na)ku** to prepare for exam.
- Students will investigate a new online thesaurus for use in future writing.

Poetry?

In Science Class?

Your brain works differently when you use it to do creative things. It builds and stores information in a different way than it does when using flashcards or other memorization techniques.

Today you will use two forms of poetry—the Sevenling and the Hay(na)ku—to review your vocabulary words;

FIGURE 5.1 Objectives and introduction slides.

Show them a Sevenling poem: "Revolution vs. Rotation" (Figure 5.2). I have provided an assortment of Sevenling and Haynakus in the Poetry Sampler, located at the end of the chapter. Choose one you like, or go online and search for Sevenling or Hay(na)ku in your subject area. They are out there, waiting to be found.

The slide that follows is from another science topic. Ask students what they notice. Noticing is an effective observation practice. They should notice the seven lines. Explain that it does not look like a "poem-y" poem. It is, however, a poem—a collection of carefully chosen words grouped to share an idea or concept. Ask them to tell you what they can learn from this poem.

Gayle: This is a Sevenling Poem. What do you notice about it? Encourage discussion (e.g., seven lines, the title, the differences between the stanzas, and the poem's information about the topic). *Notice that it does not rhyme. It doesn't have to! Is this poem factual? What does it explain about the definitions for revolution and rotation? What part of the poem is playful? Does that affect the quality of the information it provides? In what way?*

Revolution vs Rotation

Revolution: the term used to describe the Earth's orbital motion around the Sun.
Rotation: the spinning motion of the Earth on its axis.

The Circle of Life Pleases No One

Rotation—it's the same thing every *day*,
spinning around and around, over and over
I'm dizzy—could I get off this *earth*? Rev—I need a break!

Hey, Rot—you think you've got it bad—try being a **Revolution!**,
It takes me a *year* to move you around the sun—
and you're no lightweight! Stop whining!

Some planets are never happy…
GJ Sands, 2024

FIGURE 5.2 Revolution vs Rotation.

Then, show them the format of the Sevenling form and the model poems "Mitosis" and "Diffusion." Pay attention to the labels on the slide as they compare to the Sevenling form (Figures 5.3 and 5.4).

Gayle: Now we will look at the form--the arrangement of the words in the poem. Think about the poem you read with me as we review the form. This is the way the poem is organized. There is no limit to the number of words per line. They do not have to rhyme. They DO have to convey information to help you remember the meaning of the vocabulary terms. These are the only rules for the poem. You may alter the form to help demonstrate your meaning.

The Sevenling

- 7 lines
- 3 stanzas
- Stanza 1: 3 lines
- What the word means/an example
- Stanza 2: 3 lines
- a contrast—can be opposite or just different
- Stanza 3: 1 line
- Close it up with something to think about.

FIGURE 5.3 The Sevenling form.

Gayle: Here are two poems written for a biology class. Think about what we have discussed and how these poems meet the requirements for the Sevenling form. How are these poems similar? What is different? Do they define the terms?

SEVENLING: Mitosis

Mitosis: stage of cell cycle in which the nucleus divides into two new identical nuclei

Mitosis: The Final Goodbye

It has finally come. Time to split up,
to separate. There just isn't enough room ⟨ 1st Stanza; 3 lines ⟩
in this cell for both of us anymore.

We move apart slowly, carefully, with regret.
You've grown. So have I. Now we have to say goodbye. ⟨ 2nd Stanza; 3 lines ⟩
Farewell. I can see the barrier between us.

And, suddenly, we are two. Separate. Alone.
But...Look down, my friend..."My toes is"... just like your toes! ⟨ 3rd (extra) Stanza; 3 lines ⟩
We are identical!

That's Mitosis! ⟨ 4th Stanza; 1 line ⟩

Notice that I did not follow the rules here. I needed more words, so I added an extra stanza. Poetry means we can break the rules!

SEVENLING: Diffusion

Diffusion: the dispersion/spread of substances by the natural movement of their particles

Diffusion

Summer vacation--we diffuse from the school
We scatter, we spread out, we splatter ⟨ 1st Stanza; 3 lines ⟩
our smiles on the world. Life is good. Diffusion!

But remember, school awaits us.
We will reassemble, congregate, ⟨ 2nd Stanza; 3 lines ⟩
concentrate....
Diffusion must end.

⟨ 3rd Stanza; 1 line ⟩

We cannot refuse to "de-diffuse."

FIGURE 5.4 Two Sevenling Poems—Mitosis and Diffusion.

Gayle: The next form (**Figure 5.5**) *is more strict. This is a Hay(na)ku--a variation on the haiku you all know--remember, the five syllables, seven syllables, five syllables poems you have read and written? This form is based on words, not syllables. Look at the format--it goes from one word to two to three. Six words were not enough in this poem, so we reversed it--three-two-one. Besides that rule, you can write what you want if it helps us understand your terms. Notice how all of the lines explain something about microorganisms. If you need to, you can reverse it again--one-two- three. The power is in your hands.*

The Hay(na)ku

Each Stanza contains:

3 Lines and 6 words (total)

(A reversed Hay(na)ku simply turns the organization of the poem on its head for the second stanza)

- Line 1: 1 word
- Line 2: 2 words
- Line 3: 3 words

- (reverse it!)
  (no words here)

- Line 4: 3 words
- Line 5: 2 words
- Line 6: 1 word

HAY(NA)KU: Microorganism

Microorganisms: extremely small living things, made up of one or two cells (unicellular or multicellular); visible only under a microscope

Microorganism
Alive (one word)
Very tiny
Microscope for examination
Unicellular/multicellular
Everywhere!

FIGURE 5.5 Hay(na)ku structure and model (microorganism).

Task 4: Introduce the Inquiry Process

Writing poetry is inquiry work. Students have to synthesize ideas as they do so. They will generate more questions and need more language to make sense of that single conceptual word. (See Chapter 4 for using poetry with inquiry.) One resource that students need access to while writing poetry is a thesaurus. WordHippo *(WordHippo.com)* is my go-to online thesaurus.

WordHippo is user-friendly and lends itself to creativity by providing context for word definitions with an exhaustive list of synonyms, antonyms, rhyming words, and translations for almost any word or phrase you enter.

Other traditional online thesaurus sites, like *Dictionary.com, Thesaurus.com,* and *Thesaurus by Merriam-Webster,* allow students to find synonyms, similar words, and antonyms. If online access is only available for some students, go old-school with a printed thesaurus or dictionary. However, try to provide at least one online resource for the class.

Students will need access to topic-specific resources, too. As the content area expert, generate some additional sources. You might print some articles or have a diagram on the tables to help students discover additional language for making meaning. Photographs and diagrams will help students see relational concepts they can include in their poems. If a website is specific to your topic, encourage students to refer to that to make connections between terms.

In my lesson with 7th graders, I did a walk-through of *WordHippo*. I picked a term I used in my poem, opened WordHippo, and thought aloud about my search process. The screenshots and script below provide an example of my word explorations. This part of the lesson took about ten minutes, but I could have invested more in the discussion if there had not been a time issue. The website lends itself to a lively conversation as students notice quirky and exciting terms in the lists of synonyms.

As they worked, I moved from group to group, pointing out possible synonyms and suggesting how they might use them. As they searched, I encouraged them to look for connections to their personal lives and reminded them that the poems could be humorous as long as they were accurate. It took a few minutes for them to be comfortable with the website, but work moved along quickly after that.

A Few Pro Tips:

1. Set a time limit on the investigation process. Even the most on-task, conscientious group will be tempted to waste time in the rabbit hole of synonyms.
2. Remind them that they only need four or five synonyms for their final poem but that they should begin with a broader selection to be able to choose the best ones.
3. Tell them to make a rough list of all the words they consider—probably starting with eight to ten, and narrow it down once they start writing. Sometimes, a word they didn't consider will fit beautifully once they get into the poem. And they can always go back to the website for more searches.

Modeling is critical to the process. You will model the task by taking one of the vocabulary words—maybe one from a previous unit or one not assigned to a student and going through the Sevenling process. Begin with a word review, then go to WordHippo to explore word choices. Do a think-aloud about your process and the choices you are making. Show how you draw on the word, the definition, the notes you made, and the inquiry. Let me walk you through what I did with a script to help you if you are unsure what to say. I start with a quick introduction to their reference tool, WordHippo. You may choose to include other reference sources before your learners begin writing (Figure 5.6).

INTRODUCTION TO WORD HIPPO

HTTPS://WWW.WORDHIPPO.COM/

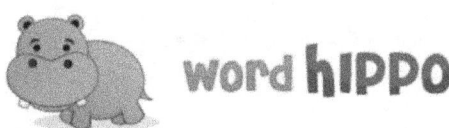

FIGURE 5.6 Introductory slide to WordHippo.

Gayle: As a starting point, I chose the vocabulary term "trait" (See Figure 5.7) for my poems. It is both a scientific term and a descriptive term for people. For instance, my husband tells me that one of my personality traits is that I talk too much. That is not scientific, but it is true. The term "trait" has a wide range of applications and connections. The slides below are a quick demonstration of the process.

Suggestion: Go to the website and play around before you present to the students. You will find out how versatile the site is.

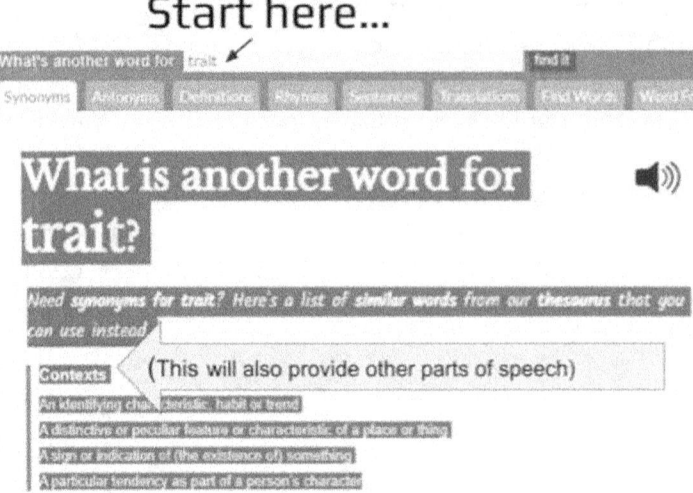

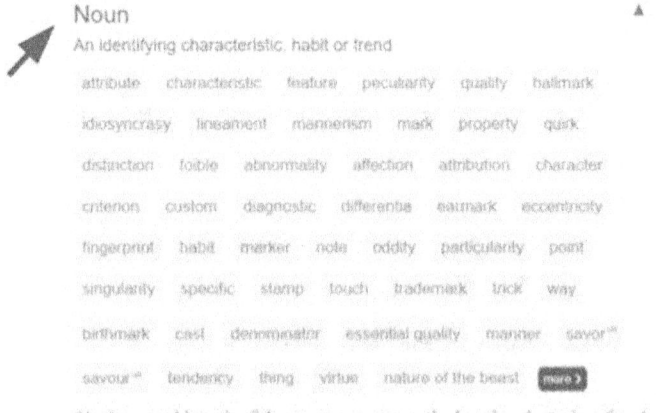

FIGURE 5.7 2 Slides WordHippo Screenshot another word for trait.

Gayle: I looked at the four contexts (meaning a frame of reference/how the term might be applied. This includes the part of speech--nouns, verbs, adjectives, etc. Many words fall into more than one category) provided by WordHippo. Trait functions only as a noun, so there were only four contexts:

- **an identifying characteristic, habit, or trend*
- ** a distinctive feature or characteristic of a place or thing*

- * a sign or indication (of the existence) of something
- *a particular tendency as part of a person's character

After scrolling quickly to check them all out for scientific and personal connections. I chose to go to the first context on the list: "An identifying characteristic, habit or trend." It seemed that I could grab some suitable synonyms for the term trait on the first scan of the screen. But I needed some more ideas.

Then I clicked on the second context, "a distinctive feature or characteristic of a place or thing," to further feed my search for exciting words for my poem. Note that scrolling to the bottom of the screen offers additional opportunities to locate alternate words for the poem (Figure 5.8).

FIGURE 5.8 Second context and additional search.

> Gayle: *I clicked on that definition and scrolled down through the synonyms. I didn't find what I wanted immediately, so I used the "more" button (bottom right) to go deeper. I made a list of all the words I found interesting/appealing: Attribute, property, essential quality, distinction, singularity, indicator, strain, quirk, oddity, knack, whim, megrim*, smidgen, smattering, sprinkle, tinge. I clicked on* megrim *to find out what it meant, in hopes that I could use it- I liked its oddness. It means a sudden change of mind or a migraine. I could use that, somehow. I wrote it down on my list of possible words to use. Clicking on megrim led me to "bee in your bonnet," "flight of fancy," and "crotchet." I liked the sound of "crotchet," a"distinctive or peculiar feature or characteristic of a place or thing." I also liked "Bee in your bonnet," so I jotted that down. I knew I could go back to the website to click on each word to read its definition.*
>
> *I knew I would try to find a way of using "crotchet' in my poem. I kept the site open so that I could go back to the list of terms later. I do not always find the "just-right" word on the first layer of synonyms or antonyms. I find the words I really like by clicking on one word and following its trail through the website.*

Pro Tip/Warning: Do NOT instruct students to just "Google it." Provide specific reference tools with their links. Google searches often lead to information that is not pertinent to your topic, may not be vetted for accuracy, and could be inappropriate. A site-specific to your lesson will yield better results and more control over the students' online actions.

> Gayle: *I had not decided what to write, so I used synonyms. I liked the word megrim and wanted words to go with it. Smidgen sounded good with it, so I returned to the term on WordHippo to find other words to use... I found maggot, mood, yen. And for smidgen, I found mite, modicum, molecule, scoosh, smitch, and smattering. Now that I have an assortment of words, I can begin writing. You can use your notebook or use the template I provided.*

The modeling process took me about ten minutes of class time. I used a poem I had written for this class and explained the steps. If you feel adventurous, you could select a word and get class input to write a spontaneous class poem as your think-aloud. Plan on this taking more than ten minutes, though. The first time you do this, it will feel intimidating. Go with it—you will go much better than you anticipate. Writing a poem is choosing strong words and lining them up to tell a story, which kids love to do.

Task 5: Provide Templates and Rubric

Some students reject graphic organizers, and others love them. Offer the option. (See the templates below—5.3 and 5.4: Template and Model Poems for Sevenling and Hy(na)ku.) You may offer students this sample template that I completed along with the blank one to provide a mentor poem from which to work. Students can do this digitally as well. You can assign the template to your learning management system (LMS), e.g., Canvas or Blackboard.

I provided a separate organizer and rubric for each poetry form before the "We-do" (Fisher & Frey, 2020) so students could follow along. As much as I would like to conserve paper, I find that students stay more focused when they have something on their desks to follow along with. I provided a separate organizer for each form, with the rubric on the back. These are provided at the end of the chapter. The bold words in the poem were taken from my research on WordHippo (Tables 5.3 and 5.4).

TABLE 5.3 Template and Model Poem for Sevenling, "The Traits Will Get You Every Time!" by G. Sands

Template for Science Sevenling
Vocabulary Word: Trait
Formal Definition: *A characteristic of a species determined by specific genes.*
Title: *The Traits Will Get You Every Time!*

Stanza 1: Three lines: description, explanation, synonyms
Line **1**. We get our **traits** from our parents, and I want to know who to blame for ME!
Line **2**. What crazy dance were their chromosomes doing?
Line **3**. A **smidgen** of this, a **scoosh** of that, a **smattering** of something else…

(Continued)

TABLE 5.3 (Continued)

Template for Science Sevenling
Vocabulary Word: Trait
Formal Definition: A characteristic of a species determined by specific genes.
Title: The Traits Will Get You Every Time!

Stanza 2: Three Lines: Contrasting/additional information about your vocabulary word
Line 4: What **bees were in the bonnets** of those particular, peculiar Punnett Squares?
Line 5: My **attributes** are an oddity; my **crotchets** combined carelessly.
Line 6: I am a **megrim** in the making.

Stanza 3: One Line: Conclusion/punch line
Line 7: I'd like to try a different combination, please.

The Traits Will Get You Every Time!
We get our traits from our parents, and I want to know who to blame for mine.
What dance did their chromosomes do to make me?
A smidgen of this, a scoosh of that, a smattering of something else…

What bees were buzzing in the bonnets of those particular Pundit Squares?
My attributes are an oddity; my crotchets combine carelessly.
I am a megrim in the making.

I'd like to try a different combination, please!
GjSands 2024

TABLE 5.4 Template and Poem Model for Hy(na)ku Poem, "Traits and Why They Matter"

Model Template for Science Hay(na)ku
Vocabulary term: Trait
Formal Definition: A characteristic of a species determined by specific genes.
Title of Poem: **Traits, and Why They Matter**

Line 1: one word	Attributes	XXXXXXXXXX	XXXXXXXXXX
Line 2: two words	Essential	qualities	XXXXXXXXXX
Line 3: three words	Make	us	individuals
REVERSE!	XXXXXXXXXX	XXXXXXXXXX	XXXXXXXXXX
Line 4: three words	Without	them,	everyone
Line 5: two words	Would	be	XXXXXXXXXX
Line 6: one word	Identical	XXXXXXXXXX	XXXXXXXXXX

Traits, and Why They Matter
Attributes,
Essential qualities
Making us individuals.

Without them everyone
would be
Identical
GJSands 2024

Ideally, you will have the time to write your own poem as a model, whether through writing one with the class or as a solo think-aloud model. It goes surprisingly quickly if you contemplate beforehand, and being part of/seeing the writing process helps your students. Try this out before you teach a class that day, but since you will likely teach the class several times, you will write several poems. You will become a poet. Congratulations!

Now, turn it over to the students.

Depending on their comfort level, you could do another poem as a large group, with students contributing and playing with the website, or you could just let them get started.

As part of your final instructions, emphasize your focus on meaning rather than structure or form of the poem. This is *your* class, not an English class! The goal is to think about the vocabulary term with a fresh viewpoint.

> Gayle: *So now it is your turn. Remember, I am not grading you on literary quality, and we will NOT be analyzing your poems, although we <u>will</u> share them. Consider all the connections to the vocabulary word you are responsible for. How can you make connections to other things in the world? How can we take the mystery out of these scientific (or math or history) words and make them comfortable and easy to remember? You may create it on your laptop or hand-write the poem. I will be grading using the rubric on the back of your organizer. Take a look at it now and make sure you understand the criteria.*

Review the rubric and the templates. Discuss whether adding another stanza or line is okay to define their vocabulary word fully. The poem is meant to offer flexibility and creativity, not to limit it. It is their poem to write.

> Gayle: *If you want to add another stanza, word, or line to the poem, go ahead. This is poetry, not punishment. Have fun with it, and be creative. Before we begin, do you have any questions?*

Set a time limit. Place a timer somewhere so students can monitor their progress against the time left in class.

> Gayle: *You have twenty minutes to create your rough draft. You may illustrate it if you like. If you do not complete it today, we will have ten minutes at the start of class tomorrow to finish it before you share it with the class.*

During this time, you can walk around and ask questions, assess student learning, point them to resources, and pose follow-up questions. If a student needs help getting started, give them support. Make a comparison or a connection that relates to the student so that they can move forward. Your observations and coaching are among the highest teaching and formative assessment forms!

Remind them to talk quietly and to make sure they are writing something. A visible timer helps here.

When I taught this lesson, one group of three students was assigned a word and were clearly having trouble getting started. I stopped by the group, discussed what they had accomplished thus far (very little), selected a few words from WordHippo, and quickly made one line of the poem for them. I also reminded them that I would check back in a couple of minutes to check their progress. They got to work.

Other groups worked quietly and efficiently. As I walked by, those groups needed quick praise. One group had an apparent power struggle. After a short discussion, I separated them so each could do their poem.

After about 20 minutes, I checked in with the class. About three-fourths of them had their rough drafts completed. Since we had used up class time for the day, we decided to complete or improve the drafts of their poems as a warm-up the following day.

Assessment

Of course, you have been assessing informally throughout the class-watching, monitoring, providing feedback and suggestions, scaffolding—all those formative assessment things we do every day, all day. Now you have student poems—the product of all that hard work. You have a summative assessment, an evaluation, or a grade—something to satisfy the gradebook. Let us look at some sample poems and the rubric I applied to them. (*How To Create and Use Rubrics for Formative Assessment and Grading*, 2013)

You can create whatever criteria you like for this rubric, but I use connections, clarity, and organization. Like every rubric and every grade, this is arbitrary and subjective. These are the factors I chose to focus on; you may choose other criteria. Ideally, you and the students will create the rubric together, but you must put numbers in the gradebook. The grade should reflect the connection between the critical vocabulary and the study of the word through the thesaurus work and writing. You may add to the rubric elements as they relate to their class notes. Consider adding a reflection such as: "How does this poem demonstrate your understanding of the word? What more do you want to learn or understand?"

Let's look at a few poems from my students. I will talk you through how I assess them using the rubric I created. Over the years, the clearer my criteria have become, the easier it has been to assess learning. You will notice that the poetic <u>form</u> is not the focus of the evaluation. The grade is based on the goal of this assignment—understanding the vocabulary and making meaningful connections to real-life processes (Tables 5.5 and 5.6).

TABLE 5.5 Simple Assessment Rubric for Vocabulary/Poetry Assignment

Criteria

Connections between poem's content and vocabulary term.	Minimal or no connections	**Connections** are attempted but may show *confusion or lack of clarity*	**Connections** between the poem and the term are *easy to understand*.	**Multiple connections** show *vital insight* into the term's meaning
Content/clarity: Writer clearly "gets" the vocabulary term	It is *difficult* to see evidence of understanding the term	Shows a *basic understanding* of the term	Shows *a good understanding* of the term with *accurate detail*.	Shows a *clear understanding* of the term with *accuracy and creativity*
Organization: Meets the requirements of chosen form or style.	Does not meet requirements.	Meets basic requirements.	Meets all requirements.	Meets and exceeds requirements, demonstrating *originality and effort*.
Comments:				

TABLE 5.6 Four Samples of Student Poetry With Grading Comments

Student Poems	Application of Rubric
A note about this student: staring at her page for five minutes while quietly working on a crochet project in her lap. She told me that she was unable to get any ideas down. Her teacher had shared with me that she crocheted to control her anxiety. I suggested that she associate the process of crocheting with how genetics is carried through generations. All it took was making a connection. Her shoulders relaxed, and she began writing this poem:	

Student Sevenling
Genetics
When I crochet
I link the yarn
one stitch at a time.
 	
Genetics
   links one generation
   to another, creating
   something new
 	
One allele at a time.
	This poem creatively **connects** genetics to crocheting in **multiple** ways (stitching=bonding, reference to alleles, generations), provides a **creative** and **accurate** example of genetics, and thoroughly meets—exceeds—all requirements as assigned.

Students' Recessive Gene Hay(na)kus What I love about these student Haynakus is their casual voice, real-world connections, and scientific accuracy. They "get it."	
Smaller Hides a lot Can skip generations Without showing up Blue eyes Sneaky	This poem **connects** the characteristics of the recessive gene in **multiple** ways: (smaller, hides, skips generations). He clearly describes its "personality" (sneaky) and provides a practical example (blue eyes).
Concealed Very unexpressed There goes recessive Hidden and quiet Inactive, sleeping Unseen	This poet understands the term. This person could be described as shy and retiring. I noted multiple connections and clearly understood the recessive gene's characteristics.
Always overpowered Hardly shows up I have faith It will Return	This simple poem makes multiple connections creatively. It does not adhere to the Haynaku pattern, but the instructions allowed the student to make changes as needed. This poem quietly makes its point in very few well-chosen words.

The three student poems in the chart were in the same word study group, but each wrote very different Hay(na)kus. They all strongly comprehended the concept but applied the information in a thoroughly individual style. That is what makes poetry so valuable—the personal connection students make (Table 5.7).

TABLE 5.7 Two Columns, Two-Line Poem About Genetics With Assessment Comments

Another Student Poem	*My suggestions for revision when conferring with the student:*
Genetics The dominant always gets the victory. The recessive always gets full-boxed and fails	* This poem references strength. **Connections** are attempted but need m*ore clarity*. I would like to know what they might write with more time. * Contains minimal detail. Did they have notes? Need more time? * The poem refers to the topic but does not follow either of the forms assigned, so what support can I offer?

Task 6: Share the Knowledge

As you observe their writing, whether students are comfortable with their assigned term will be clear. However, knowledge of one word does not prepare them for the test. Every student needs to learn *all* the words. The good news is that as each poet presents their poem; they provide creative and multi-pronged ways to learn and remember the words on the list.

Students can learn/review the rest of the words in several ways. The simplest method is to have each group/student present their term's formal definition and poem. Students should take notes on the terms in their notebooks/worksheets with ideas that will help them recall definitions later. My friend shared the poems with the ELA teacher on her team, who celebrated them in her class—two reviews for one activity! The chart below provides other ways to celebrate the students' work (Table 5.8).

TABLE 5.8 Poetic Celebrations: An Assortment of Possible Ways to Share the Poems With the Class

Poetic Celebrations

Poetry Quilt: This is an upscale word wall. It is an excellent idea for parent visitation night—Google "classroom quilt template" for printouts and instructions. Many are available for free.
- Students copy vocabulary poems onto colored paper (decorated as you and the students see fit) and assemble them as quilts.
- Post the "quilt" in the classroom or the hallway, sharing the vocabulary with everyone walking by.
- You can add to it as topics change or create a new "quilt" for each unit, rotating or switching them as desired.

(Continued)

TABLE 5.8 (Continued)

Poetic Celebrations

Vocabulary Slam: Each student shares their poem with the class. Finger clicks of approval make it "cool." Think about turning it into an old-school coffee shop atmosphere. Google "classroom poetry slam" for ideas.
- Remind students to be respectful to ALL presenters.
- Provide an off-ramp for students who are uncomfortable reading aloud by designating a "pinch-reader" to present the drafts of their classmate's poem.
- If multiple groups have the same word, you may have groups with the term share their poems and discuss the concept behind them. Then, move on to another term/group. Students will receive multiple opportunities to think about each term.
- Encourage dramatic readings of their poems. Provide an example with a dramatic delivery of your poem.

What's My Word? Students/groups share poems without stating the title or the vocabulary word; the class guesses the word. This could be done as a team or individual contest.
- Set up teams based on the writing groups
- Provide a form for individual students to use (See Table 5.13)
- Set up teams by random selection. One rule to enforce is that the team/person who wrote the poem must recuse themselves from that poem.
- Assign a number to each poem for recording terms.
- Depending on your class, you may read them aloud so students keep the answers private.
- Offer small prizes to the winning team or individual.

Cooperative Slide Show: Create a shared digital slide presentation to review the words with the class before a quiz.
- Create a master presentation to share with students. Each student adds their poem to the presentation as a separate slide. They may add visuals if they choose.

Gallery Walk: Display the poems so students can see what others have written.
- Place individual poems around the edges of the room. To avoid traffic jams, start each group of observers at a different poem and have them move around to each poem • each group moves to the right to view the next poem.
- Provide a positive comment sheet on or near each poem for students to fill out. Provide sentence starters such as "I liked; This connects to; This reminds me of; The best part is."

Conclusion

Congratulations. You have made it to the end of the chapter, and I only made you worry about three (maybe four?) terms in literature/poetry. You will find that it is worth the additional investment of class time to write poetry that helps to lock in the vocabulary terms our students need to comprehend the text. Poetry is another way—a humanizing way—to build knowledge. It offers a creative approach to organizing ideas, thoughts, and meaning. It is one more strategy to help your students apply and retain what they have learned. It takes student learning beyond decoding and memorization to the creation of real meaning as it relates to our students' lives. It's worth the time investment. Try it—you will like it!

SUPPORT MATERIALS
LESSON PLAN TEMPLATE

TABLE 5.9 Lesson Template: Tasks on the Left and Discussion/Extension on the Right

Basic Lesson Plan Template

Task 1: Choose the Words	Discussion/Application: Science
Create the vocabulary list: Determine the essential vocabulary for your lesson. Decide which terms MUST be understood and which would be "nice to know." For this deep dive into understanding, choose the terms that offer the most power to your lesson.	**Key terms:** Based on the focus of my lesson, which is the understanding of the Punnett Square as a predictor of the results of genetic crosses 1. Probability 2. Punnett square 3. Phenotype 4. Genotype 5. Dominant 6. Recessive 7. Codominance 8. Gene
Present the vocabulary list to students: Provide a handout and an online list with the vocabulary words they will choose from. This should consist of all the terms you want them to learn. Include the following on the handout: 1) The **term** and its variations (if they exist); 2) The **formal definition** (probably from your text).	Note--possible variations follow the definition **Probability:** a number that describes how likely it is that an event will occur (probable, probably) **Punnett square:** Chart that shows the possible outcomes of a genetic cross **Phenotype:** An organism's physical appearance; visible trait **Genotype:** An organism's genetic makeup/allele combinations (genotypical) **Dominant:** the gene whose trait always shows up when the gene/allele is present (dominate)

(Continued)

TABLE 5.9 (Continued)

Basic Lesson Plan Template

	Recessive: an allele that is masked when a dominant allele is present (recess, recede) **Gene:** set of information that controls an organism's trait (genetics, genealogy, genetically) **Trait:** A characteristic of a species determined by specific genes.
Review the *context* for each vocabulary term as it applies to your topic. This should be done as a group, whether through group discussion or via slide presentation. Students should take notes on all terms. This ensures they understand the terms and reduces confusion later on. This *formative assessment* sets the class up for success.	**Sample note-taking format:** Name: Term: Formal definition: What it really means: Why I should care about it:

Task 2: Assign the Terms (Who Gets What?) /Application

Before you begin: Pairs, groups, or solo work?	• You know your class—decide how you want them to interact. I have found that a group larger than three results in more socialization than productive writing. • If a student wants to work alone, let them. Although discussion is productive, it is not required.
Assign terms: You will need to assign each term to more than one group. It will be surprising to see how the poems vary using the same vocabulary term.	**Assignment alternatives** • You assign them. No student choice • Use popsicle sticks/grab-bag to determine who picks first, second… • Use an online randomizer to assign words OR to determine the chosen order. A free online source is <u>Wheel of Names</u>.

Task 4: Introduce Poetry. Provide purpose, background, process, and examples.

Present and review slides for modeling; a model by creating a new poem	**See:** * sample slides: Figures 5.1–5.5 * accompanying script

TABLE 5.9 (Continued)

Basic Lesson Plan Template

Task 4: Provide Research Tools /Application	
WordHippo www.wordhippo.com/ is my go-to online thesaurus.	See: *sample slides: Figures 5.6–5.8 *accompanying script WordHippo is user-friendly and lends itself to creativity by providing context for word definitions with an exhaustive list of synonyms, antonyms, rhyming words, and translations for almost any word or phrase entered.
Traditional online thesaurus sites	Dictionary.com Thesaurus.com, Thesaurus by Merriam-Webster: Find Synonyms, Similar Words, and Antonyms
If online access is not available for all students…	You can go old-school with a printed thesaurus or dictionary. However, try to provide at least one online resource for the group.
Topic-specific resources	If a website is specific to your topic, encourage students to refer to that to make connections between terms.
Task 5: Provide Organizers & Grading Rubric/Application	
Sample organizers/rubric follow.	I provided students with a separate organizer and rubric for each poetry form before the "We-do" so they could follow along. As much as I would like to conserve paper, I find that students stay more focused when they have something on their desks to follow along with.
Task 6: Share the Poems for Class Review/Celebration	
Provide an opportunity for students to share poems and discuss the terms they wrote about	Students should review all the terms assigned to the class by sharing them with the group. Table 5.8 contains a list of suggestions for extending the project.

Sevenling Instructions and Organizer

Student Instructions:

1. Provide the formal definition at the beginning of your poem
   Think of examples and non-examples OR opposites to the word/concept.
2. Use a thesaurus to stretch your thinking. Consider all synonyms/antonyms you could use. Go to www.wordhippo.com for inspiration. Explore the site—it may give you a new direction.
3. Consider all forms of the word as you research and write--nouns, verbs, adjectives, and adverbs.
4. Create a title for your work. Illustrate it if you choose to do so.

Vocabulary Word: _____
Formal Definition: _____

Title: (Include your vocabulary word): _____

TABLE 5.10 Sevenling Organizer/Template for Student Use

Stanza 1: Three lines: description, explanation, synonyms

Line 1.

Line 2.

Line 3.

Stanza 2: Three Lines: Contrasting/additional information about your vocabulary word

Line 4:

Line 5:

Line 6:

Stanza 3: One Line: Conclusion/punch line

Line 7:

Hay(na)ku Instructions and Organizer

The Hay(na)ku has three lines, with six words: one word in the first, two in the second, and three in the third. You can also add a reverse Hay(na)ku (three words, two words, one word)

1. Write down words or phrases that connect to the vocabulary word. They do not need to be "academic" words-- use the words/ideas that make sense to *you*.
2. Make a list of words/phrases that explain your term.
3. Choose the words that best explain your term. You will probably have to sort it down more than once—you are going for the essence of the term's meaning. *(Think of a funnel--only the best words should make it through to the poem.)*
4. Use the organizer to structure your poem.

HAY(NA)KU ORGANIZER

Vocabulary term: _____
Formal Definition: _____

Title of Poem: _____

TABLE 5.11 Hay(na)ku Organizer/Template for Student Use

Line 1: one word		XXXXXXXXXX	XXXXXXXXXX
Line 2: two words			XXXXXXXXXX
Line 3: three words			
REVERSE!	XXXXXXXXXX	XXXXXXXXXX	XXXXXXXXXX
Line 4: three words			
Line 5: two words			XXXXXXXXXX
Line 6: one word		XXXXXXXXXX	XXXXXXXXXX

Grading Rubric (Copy on the back of worksheet)

TABLE 5.12 Grading Rubric for Poetry Assignment

Criteria				
Connections between poem's content and vocabulary term.	Minimal or no connections	**Connections** are attempted but may show *confusion or lack of clarity*	**Connections** between the poem and the term are *easy to understand.*	**Multiple connections** show *vital insight* into the term's meaning
Content/clarity: Writer clearly "gets" the vocabulary term	It is *difficult* to see evidence of understanding the term	Shows a *basic understanding* of the term	Shows a *good understanding* of the term with *accurate detail.*	Shows a *clear understanding* of the term with *accuracy and creativity*
Organization Meets the requirements of chosen form or style.	Does not meet requirements.	Meets basic requirements.	Meets all requirements.	Meets and exceeds requirements, demonstrating *originality and effort.*
Comments:				

TABLE 5.13 What's My Word Template

What's My Word?
List of vocabulary words assigned:

Student Name:	Number of the poems you wrote:
Poem Number Vocabulary topic/term	The most helpful clue in the poem

1.

2.

Poetry Applications for the Non-ELA Classroom: Original Poems for Science, Math, Social Sciences and World Languages
By Gayle Sands
Sevenlings and Hay(na)kus:

Science
Sevenling: Revolution vs Rotation
Revolution "refers to the object's orbital motion around another object."
Rotation "refers to an object's spinning motion about its own axis."
National Aeronautics and Space Administration (n.d.). "Chapter 2: Reference Systems – Rotation and Revolution." *NASA Science*,

> *The Circle of Life Pleases No One*
>
> Rotation--it's the same thing every *day*,
> spinning around and around, over and over
> I'm dizzy--could I get off this *earth*? I need a break!
>
> Hey, Rot--you think you've got it bad--try being the
>   *earth's* revolution!
> It takes me a *year* to move you around the sun.
> Then I get to do it all over again. And you're no lightweight!

Some planets are never happy.
GJSands 2024

Mitosis: Stage of cell cycle in which the nucleus divides into two new identical nuclei

Mitosis

> It has finally come. Time to split up,
> to separate. There just isn't enough room
> in this cell for both of us anymore.
>
> We move apart slooowly, carefully, with regret.
> You grew. So did I. Now we have to say goodbye.
> Farewell. I can see the barrier between us.
>
> And, suddenly, we are two. Separate. Alone.
> But…Look down, my friend…"*My toes is*"… just like
>   your toes!
> We are identical! That's **Mitosis!**
> GJS 2024

Reversed Hay(na)ku
Phenotype: feature or quality that serves to identify an organism

> Look
> You see
> Tall, short, tiny
> Blonde, brown hair
> All different
> Everyone!
> Genetics
> (student) 2024

Math Sevenling
(actually, it is more of a "nineling" due to having three terms that are closely related)

Mean: the arithmetic average
Mode: the number(s) or item(s) that appear most often in a data set
Median: the middle number of a data set when numbers are arranged in numerical order

Mean, Median, and Mode

The "mode" for finding the *mode* is simple
Just look for the most, the preponderance, the lion's share.
The mode roars the loudest because there are more of them in the group.

Look in the middle for the *median*. They live halfway,
never near the beginning or the end. Never! Centermost, middlemost.
They are happy where they are-right in the middle of things.

The **mean** is not really cruel. It doesn't deserve its reputation.
It gathers all the numbers together in one big group,
then divides them equally. It's very fair.

The **mean** is a really big deal, though. It determines your grade in math class!
GJS 2024

Math Hay(na)ku
Probability: The chance that some event will happen; the ratio of the number of ways something can occur to the number of possible outcomes

Probability
Likelihood
Event's occurrence
Possible occurrences divided
By total possibilities
The ratio
Percentage
GJS 2024

Social Studies
(Check out History for Kids, which has a number of examples of history-based poetry)

> **Sevenling: Lucy**
> Lucy (*https://iho.asu.edu/about/lucys-story*)
> Terms: Hominid, Lucy, Remains
>
> They found Lucy's bones in Africa.
> Her *remains* remained hidden for millions of years
> Scientists called her "southern ape."
>
> Lucy was no leftover *hominid*. She was important!
> She walked on two feet so she could use her hands
> Her *remains* have taught us about the first *humanoids*.
>
> Lucy's bones may have been small, but her *remains* are a really big deal.
> GJS. 2024

Sevenling: Migration
Late Pleistocene Facts for Kids

> **Migrators**
> Our Pleistocene ancestors were serious *migrators*.
> They vamoosed. They split. They evacuated.
> They walked out and kept walking. They MOVED.

Sedentary settlers stay in one place.
They stay. They dwell. They linger. They definitely do not *migrate*.
They hang around. They sit tight. They put down roots.

Not these ancestors. *They* were like the Rolling Stones.
They *migrated*.
GJS 2024

Sevenling: Monarchy vs Democracy
"A monarchy is a form of government that has a single person known as a monarch at its head"(monarchy – Kids | Britannica Kids | Homework Help)

"The word democracy describes a form of government. The word comes from two Greek words that mean 'rule by the people.' In a democracy, the people have a say in how the government is run." (democracy – Students | Britannica Kids | Homework Help)

Monarchy vs. Democracy
I am the king here. The boss. The ruler.
Don't mess with me--this is a *monarchy*!
I am in charge, and I want it to stay that way.

Hey, King! What about us? The opinions in our *democracy* are important!
We, the citizens, the people, matter! We live here, too.
We should have a say-- every day. It's better that way!

We choose *democracy*. Let's vote. Today!
Gjs 2024

Confucianism and Daoism
Confucianism: a Chinese belief system that focuses on "kindness, love, and respect" (see Britannica Kids).[1]

Lead
by example
Just and peaceful
Respect and obey
Honor elders
Honesty
GJS 2024

Daoism: a Chinese belief focused on harmony with nature's way and maintaining balance in everything

Simple
Nature's way
Yin and Yang
Shaded and sunlit
Balance opposites
Acceptance
GJS 2024

Foreign Language and Poetry

Word Hippo provides a wide range of language translations and synonyms in addition to the English terms provided. It offers audio readings of each word in a wide variety of languages. Use the dropdown to translate target words to and from English to any language.

Frustration
(all by GJSands, 2024)

TABLE 5.14 Two Poems, One Spanish and One French, Topic: Frustration

Spanish	Yo estoy frustrada derrotada, vencida, batida. defeated, losing, beaten I am Frustrated.
French	Je suis Frustré, Découragé, désappointé, réprimé Discouraged, disappointed, repressed I am Frustrated

Student Samples Spring 2023

Reverse Hy(na)ku: Offspring
Offspring
The Kiddiewinks
Of P1 generation
the younglings that
the parents
made
C
	Sevenling: Phenotypes
	The features and qualities that make
	   you, YOU!
	Brown hair, freckles, eyes of blue
	Endless possibilities from a set of two
	
	Big B, little b is your genotype
	But people compliment your
	   phenotype
	Oh, yes, they do!
	
	We only see your phenotype!
	T and H

Reverse Hy(na)ku: Dominant On the throne Master In control Noteworthy Number one Transcendent J	Reverse Hy(na)ku: Recessive Recessive Lurking under The dominant trait But it's always Ready to Show A

Note

1   https://kids.britannica.com/kids/article/Confucius/35299

References

Beck, I. L., McKeown, M. G., & Kucan, L. (2002). *Bringing words to life: Robust vocabulary instruction*. Guilford Press.

Democracy. (n.d.). In *Britannica Kids*. Encyclopaedia Britannica. https://kids.britannica.com/students/article/democracy/273962

Doubet, K. J. (2022). *Improving student collaboration with flexible grouping* (Quick et al.). ASCD.

Fisher, D., & Frey, N. (2020). *Better learning through structured teaching: A framework for the gradual release of responsibility* (3rd ed.). ASCD.

Herrera, S. G., Kavimandan, D. R., & Holmes, M. A. (2011). *Crossing the vocabulary bridge: Differentiated strategies for diverse secondary classrooms*. Teachers College Press.

Laozi. (1988). *Dao De Jing* (S. et al.). Harmony Books.

https://kids.kiddle.co/Late_Pleistocene

Lumsden, R. (2004). *Mischief Night: New & selected poems*. Bloodaxe Books.

Marzano, R. J. (2004). *Building background knowledge for academic achievement: Research on what works in schools*. Association for Supervision and Curriculum Development.

National Aeronautics and Space Administration. (n.d.). Chapter 2: Reference systems–Rotation and revolution. *NASA Science*. https://science.nasa.gov/learn/basics-of-space-flight/chapter2-1/#h-rotation-and-revolution

Richardson, J. S., Morgan, R. F., & Fleener, C. E. (2009). *Reading to learn in the content areas* (7th ed.). Cengage Learning.

Roe, B. D., Smith, S. H., & Burns, P. C. (2015). *Secondary school literacy instruction: The content areas* (10th ed.). Cengage Learning.

Silberman, M. (2006S). *Teaching actively: Eight steps and 32 strategies to spark learning in any classroom*. Pearson.

Tabios, E. R. (2005). *Hay(na)ku*. Meritage Press.

Vacca, R. T., & Vacca, J. A. L. (2002). *Content area reading: Literacy and learning across the curriculum* (8th ed.). Allyn and Bacon.

Williams, W. C. (1944). Introduction to *the wedge*. In *Selected essays* (pp. 256–257). New Directions.

6

Summative Assessment
Demonstrating Learning as a Poetry Expo

Kim Johnson

As a public school district literacy specialist, I often participate in reflective conversations on instructional frameworks in which the phrases "summative assessment" and "formative assessment" are frequently used. Educators use these terms to describe how they gauge student learning throughout a unit of study or at the conclusion. Formative assessment helps guide instruction planning to ensure that students grasp concepts and enduring understandings they should master before the summative assessment at the end of a unit of study.

I like to think of these forms of assessment as dance lessons. The formative assessment in a dance class happens as an instructor teaches each step or sequence of steps before moving on to the following sequence. The dancing recital, or performance of the dance as it has been mastered in short bursts, is all put together for the summative assessment. Classroom instruction is similar to learning the steps of a dance routine as students move through a unit of study.

So, what can a summative assessment do? We, the educators collaborating on this book, have described ways writing and talking about poetry can help students uncover content area meaning as they compose a text that carries their new knowledge of content. Students can create new texts worthy of study as they demonstrate their learning. What do we do with the poetry our students write during a unit of instruction?

In this chapter, I offer the Student Poetry Expo as a community-based, celebratory experience that centers students' voices and learning while providing another space for education and exchanging ideas. I have used pseudonyms for student poets throughout the chapter.

The Story Behind Our Poetry Expo

In 2019, our rural school district in middle Georgia started a Humanities Pathway for our 8th-grade students entering high school in 2020. We created an interest-based elective class at our middle school so that students could engage in a 9-week *taste-and-see* experience that allowed them a glimpse of the content, mission, and vision of the courses that would comprise the high school pathway.

We opened the cohort to 20 8th-grade students who had taken the elective class and filled the first freshman cohort pathway with students eager to make the world a better place by becoming familiar with the United Nations Sustainable Goals and examining their impact on global practices.

In each unit, one of the United Nations Goals (n.d.) becomes the basis of the content. In the Genocide Unit, students delve into Goal 16 – *Promote peaceful and inclusive societies for sustainable development, provide access to justice for all, and build effective, accountable, and inclusive institutions at all levels.* Students are provided a list of books to choose from as their core reading for the unit, in addition to the anchor text, *Night,* by Elie Wiesel (2006). We formed book clubs from the core selections: *Escape from Camp 14* by Blaine Harden (2012); *The Cat I Never Named* by Amra Sabic-El-Rayess and Laura L. Sullivan (2020); *Over a Thousand Hills I Walk with You* by Hanna Jansen (2006); *Never Fall Down* by Patricia McCormick (2012); and *Nobody's Child* by Marsha Forchuk (1991). Students discussed the aspects of the United Nations Goals in the context and perspectives of their selected reading. Shorter texts, such as essays and poems, are also used. Throughout the unit, students discuss the ten stages of genocide (Stanton, 1996), define each, and provide examples and prevention.

In addition to the Holocaust, during the 1930s-40s under Adolf Hitler students also study these events:

- Armenia Genocide
- Bosnia Genocide
- Cambodia Genocide
- Darfur Genocide
- Genocide of Native Americans
- Genocide in Rwanda
- Guatemala Genocide
- Myanmar Genocide
- Ukraine Holodomor

Throughout the Humanities pathway, students keep Literary Art Journals, which contain drawings, quotes, poems, and other artistic expressions that reflect their thinking about world issues. Students were working on these in their current unit of study, but the teacher desired a common assessment (Figures 6.1-6.3).

FIGURE 6.1 Justice Art Journal with Statue of Liberty.

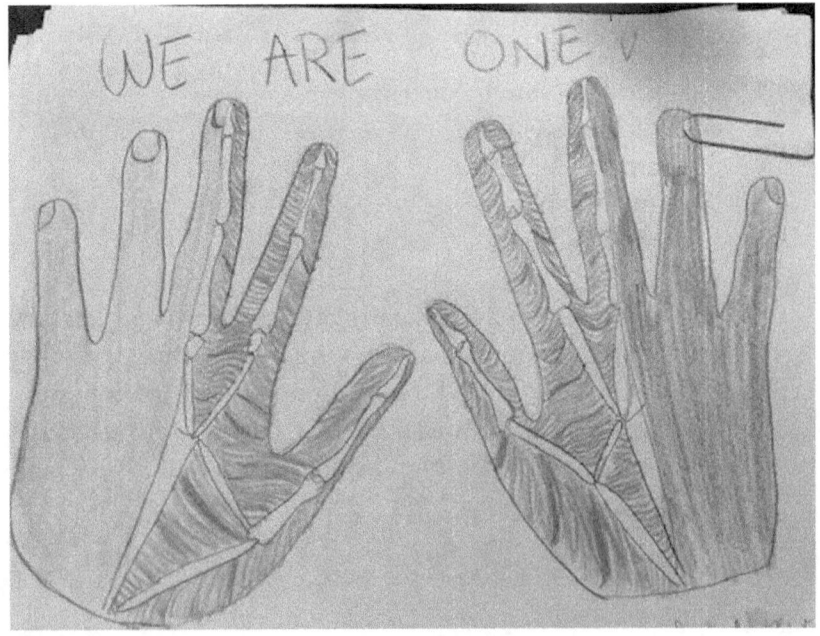

FIGURE 6.2 Equality art journal entry with hands.

FIGURE 6.3 Kindness Art Journal Entry with Ladder.

Enter Poetry

As National Poetry Month began in April 2023, I was preparing some short video tutorials on how to write various poems so that community members could visit one of several poetry kiosks and workshops throughout our town and write a poem to share on a community Padlet. One of the teachers in our Humanities pathway contacted me to ask whether I would be willing to come in and work with students to write poems for their Student Learning Expo after their unit on genocide. As a published poet in four anthologies and a childhood memoir, in addition to being a lifelong poet enthusiast and a frequent host and participant for the Open Write and #VerseLove for the past nine years at www.ethicalela.com, I embraced the invitation to this unique experience in the classroom and savored writing alongside this remarkable group of students.

By providing an opportunity for students to share what they have learned in their chosen aspect of study in a particular unit, teachers empower students' creativity even within the boundaries of content-area learning. Students who feel a great sense of reluctance and anxiety about writing *another 5-paragraph essay* (Gustafson, 2021) will dive more eagerly into the emotional investment of writing a poem they will treasure for a lifetime. Even students who do not consider themselves creative or identify themselves as writers will develop a strong sense of ownership of their work as they begin writing poetry. See these anonymized student reflections.

- Hannah reflected that "writing poetry helped me look into other aspects of genocide nobody thinks of," further explaining that "this experience helped me write something from my past onto paper and incorporate my own life into writing, along with the courage to open up."
- Raul shared that he enjoyed piecing together the personal experiences of many into "one big story and making it my own," noting poetry allowed the creativity to allow the words to flow onto the paper.
- Kalen shared, "Poetry helped me channel all of the stone-cold facts together from the perspective of a person, helping me feel connected to the victims and giving me a better understanding of what they endured." Her experience helps illustrate what Vazquez (2023) found: "Poetry has a unique capacity for enabling us to bear the vicissitudes of human existence (55)."

From Reading to Writing Poetry: Synthesizing Learning

While students read poems about genocide throughout the unit as shorter texts that connect to the longer anchor text, we reserved our invitation for students to compose their poetry until the conclusion so that they would have a collection of memorable learning experiences from which to choose as they wrote their poems.

For this unit, our Humanities teachers incorporated poetry writing after spending six weeks learning about their chosen topic as they prepared for the student expo. Students began writing poetry the week before the expo and showcased their poems at the kiosks that they set up to reflect on their learning with stakeholders who attended the expo. Because the students' poetry exhibited the summative experience, a culmination of their collective learning and sharing throughout the unit, it provided more than just one way to summarize and synthesize their learning; it also provided a way for students to display their insights and react to their discoveries. Parents, community members, extended family members, administrators from other schools, and our teachers attended the expo. They expressed their awe at the deeper learning when students were invited to express their learning through poems.

Providing students an opportunity to choose from various poetic forms to share their learning and express their feelings ensures that every student can experience success as they think critically about their learning and express their understandings and feelings in their own words. Students' learning bloomed through paint chip poems, free verse, Where I'm From poems, Jenga block poems, and Cento poems. I modeled how to write one of each, using the short videos I had created on YouTube for community members. Students chose their preferred style and began writing poems using the context of their unit of study as their empathetic lens.

Now, let's shift our focus to the steps teachers can take to bring a poetry expo to a classroom and the greater community. I'll walk you through the process, step by step, from preparation to process to poetic celebration.

Preparing for the Expo

Step 1: Study Mentor Texts

One poem the teacher shared and that they read with partners and individually to experience poetry as an emotion-charged primary source document during the unit was *The Butterfly* by Pavel

Friedmann, which was written at Theresienstadt concentration camp on June 4, 1942. At least two versions of *The Butterfly* exist in different translations[1]. In September 1944, Friedmann was deported to Auschwitz, where he was killed. Poetry written by those who experienced an atrocity are primary source documents that use vocabulary and figurative language rooted in the emotional experiences of victims or survivors; these offer small windows into the minds and hearts of the writers there. Students also researched other poetry of genocide and discovered poems that spoke to them.

Step 2: Flipping Poetic Inquiry
To kick off a poetry writing experience for students as part of the culminating student expo, teachers may begin by showing students YouTube videos on different types of poetry. I have provided some links that I used to introduce poetic form, but a search of videos will also provide similar foundational processes. Students can watch the videos before or during class. Providing several poetic formats that scaffold the levels of writing support is essential so that each student sees poetry as accessible. Those who need more significant levels of support or who are reluctant writers will find success with Cento Poetry, which is comprised entirely of existing lines of poetry. Those who embrace challenge and desire more creativity in the writing experience may opt for Free Verse or Paint Chip poetry. Students somewhere in the middle may find success in a template-style poem such as Where I'm From poetry, which also allows writers to allow victims of genocide to become the speaker, thus bringing a unique voice to the writing. Offering a variety of choices ensures that each student will find a comfortable writing experience where everyone experiences writing success.

Cento Video[2]
Paint Chip Video[3]
Jenga Block Video[4]
Free Verse Poems[5]
Where I'm From Poems[6]

The Process
Step 3: Writing Poetry
Poems can be finished in two 50-minute class periods. After spending approximately 5 minutes on the first day introducing each of the five forms of poetry (total = 25 minutes) and sharing a think-aloud process of the journey of the teacher's own poetry writing experience (10-15 minutes), a teacher may then invite students to select the type of poem to write from the choices below. Day 2 will be spent writing the poems. Invite students to spend some time gathering creative thoughts before the next class period and thinking about how they would like to craft their poems. A student who felt drawn to a victim they studied may choose to become the voice of that person in a Where I'm From poem, while a student who doesn't know where to begin or who lacks ideas may choose a Cento or Jenga block poem so that they have scaffolds in place to empower their writing. See Table 6.1 of Poetry Forms below.

TABLE 6.1 Poetry Forms

	Cento	Paint Chip	Where I'm From	Free Verse	Jenga Block
Materials needed	Tongue Depressors with lines of existing poetry written on each (use a variety of poems on the theme); paper; pencils;	Either paint samples from stores or a purchased box of paint chip colors at the link below (*); paper; pencils	Template form for Where I'm From poem, accessible here: www.bu.edu/dos/files/2020/11/I-am-From-conversation-generation-exercise.pdf	paper; pencil	Jenga (**) blocks with unit theme-related words either written in permanent ink or cut from magazines and glued onto the blocks
Definition	a poem comprised of lines from existing poetry arranged into a new poem	a poem that uses names of colors on paint chips to create tone and mood through visual imagery and description	a poem that uses the voice and experiences of characters or people to provide insight into their lives through rich detail, a variation from the original by George Ella Lyon	a poem written with no rules or set structure, often originating as stream-of-consciousness writing	a poem comprised of words taken from Jenga blocks
Stanzas	unlimited	unlimited	follows template	unlimited	unlimited
Lines	unlimited	unlimited	follows template	unlimited	unlimited; may be one-word where Jenga block words stand alone, or students may use Jenga block words as a word bank and add their own words to each line

Summative Assessment: Demonstrating Learning as a Poetry Expo ◆ 193

	Cento	Paint chip	Where I Am From	Free verse	Jenga block
Rhythm	varies by lines selected and ordered/reordered	varies	follows template	varies by student choice in creating the poem	may seem choppy if one-word lines are used, but will vary by student choice in creating the poem
Repetition Schemes	varies by lines selected and ordered/reordered	varies by student choice	the template has a repetition of "I'm From."	varies by student choice	may have repetition if students choose to use words more than once
Purpose: What can this form do? What topics does it lend itself to?	Cento lends itself to any topic, provided the lines selected are from a base of poems on the subject; Cento can make all writers successful since the poem lines are chosen from lines already written and not left to the writer to begin from scratch.	Paint chip poems lend themselves to any topic, especially as the colors are selected to reflect the mood and tone of the poem, giving it emotion through visual imagery of color. Paint chip poems lend themselves to writers who think artistically and can notice parallels between color and situation.	Where I Am From poems lend themselves to expressing deep knowledge of a character or person by providing a template that inspires writers to think about the real or imagined experiences from a first-person point of view by putting themselves in the speaker's place. Where I'm From poems can empower students to be successful poets by walking a mile in another's shoes.	Free verse poems lend themselves to the ultimate creative writing experiences, ranging from stream-of-consciousness writing to blending several types of poems with differing structures. They can enable students to select a point of view and experiment with taking their audible thoughts and breaking them into lines to form poems along a wide range of possibilities.	Jenga block poems build mood and vocabulary by focusing on unit-related words on a given topic. These poems provide a moderately reluctant writer with the words to get started and lend themselves to any topic for which teachers have created a word bank of Jenga blocks.

Students can begin drafting their poems once they have seen a variety of formats presented as options either on YouTube or modeled by a teacher. A sample of each type of poetry being shared helps serve as a mentor text for the type of poetry from which students may choose, and a poem such as "The Butterfly" by Pavel Friedmann is one example of a theme-related mentor text for the genocide unit.

To guide students to the starting point of their writing, ask them to choose the type of poem they would like to write and then write an expression or reaction to their discoveries throughout the unit in a poetic form. Teachers may decide to write a poem ahead of time and jot notes about their thinking in order to guide students through a think-aloud process, where they hear their teacher talk through the poetry writing process and witness the productive struggle of writing as they see the pride that comes with ownership of the process.

Here is a Cento poem entitled "Remember," written by a student who took the voice of a survivor and discovered a voice of activism in the existing lines of poetry she arranged to compose her poem.

Remember by Hannah

Crushing my teeth from my terrible rage
to kiss the last of my world
let it bleed in the street until morning
It's hard to love without you
I stand and fight against genocide today
We who survived will remember you
Victims of war and genocide
No, I do not want to remember
but I cannot forget
Let us remember how the law failed us
Unaware of love affairs to us
I saw with my cruel human eyes
A horizon without sorrow
Children shaking like leaves in the wind
Cries of the wounded, begging for life
But I found my people here

A future spread with colors
by lack of justice for survivors
Here ends our pain
I survived!

The class collection of poems on genocide shares the students' understanding of injustice. In this poem, the line *Let us remember how the law failed us* illuminates the fervent desire to live amid struggle, further emphasized by the line *Cries of the wounded, begging for life*. Poetry can be used to issue a call to action to stand for justice, which is the poem's overall message (*I stand and fight against Genocide today*). As students share their poems with others in the class, school, and greater community, those who read or listen realize that not only did students learn about atrocities that occurred throughout history, but also that they developed a sense of passion and responsibility to share the lessons that these events teach us.

The examples below are Jenga Block poems. One Jenga poem shows words from blocks that stand alone, while the other shows how the student used a bank of words selected from the block supply to create her poem from those words and her own. In the first example, the poet was empowered to write a poem that shows an understanding of genocide without ever lifting a pencil. In the second example, the student uses Jenga blocks to create a free verse poem by using the blocks as ideas and expanding through her own words to show that a five-year-old was separated from a mother who told him the world was a dangerous place because of his culture. When offered with scaffolded support, forms of poetry enable each student to be successful as instructional strategies meet them where they are as students.

Untitled Jenga poem
by Steven
The toughest
Conquer
The fight
History Knows
United

Power
Prepared
Extreme
Stress
One world
Alone

Potential   Memorializing
Unleashed   Stories
A life without   Sparkly life
Hope

"Last Words," a Jenga poem by Julie (words in bold taken from Jenga blocks)

Last Words

Five years old is quite **young** to be **departed** from your **family**
Unfortunately, I'm all alone and **lost**
Before my parents left,
My mother told me the **world** was a dangerous place,
And that I had to hide myself from the Nazis because of my **culture**
It made no sense to me
She also **promised one day** the Nazis would be defeated and the world changed
But for **now,** I was in **danger** and I had to **fight** with **every last breath**
Her last words were that she **loved me forever.**
Those words **comforted** me for the next couple of years of my life.
But I didn't know that, that night would be my last moment with my family ever again.
Those words will give me confidence and hope, **endlessly** for the rest of my life.

Where I'm From poems, as seen in the examples below, allow students to bring a voice from a victim's life to the page through poetry to help understand that victims were people with stories and life histories, just as we are today. Teachers see through poetic tribute that students understand the mass casualties and human lives lost to atrocities (Figure 6.4).

I am From a Worn-out Prayer Shawl by Elizabeth

I am from a worn-out prayer shawl
From ink-stained diary and scented soap

Solitude, fear, scent of rain
I am from the petals of a yellow flower
Its bloom of beauty
I'm from sharing stories around the table and resilience
From Uncle David and Grandma Esther
I'm from the kitchen table gatherings and enjoying each other's presence
From tales of survival and standing up for what's right
I'm from faith passed down, connection greater than us
I'm from cobblestone streets of our town
Matzo ball soup, freshly baked challah
From the Great Grandfather Isaac's story.

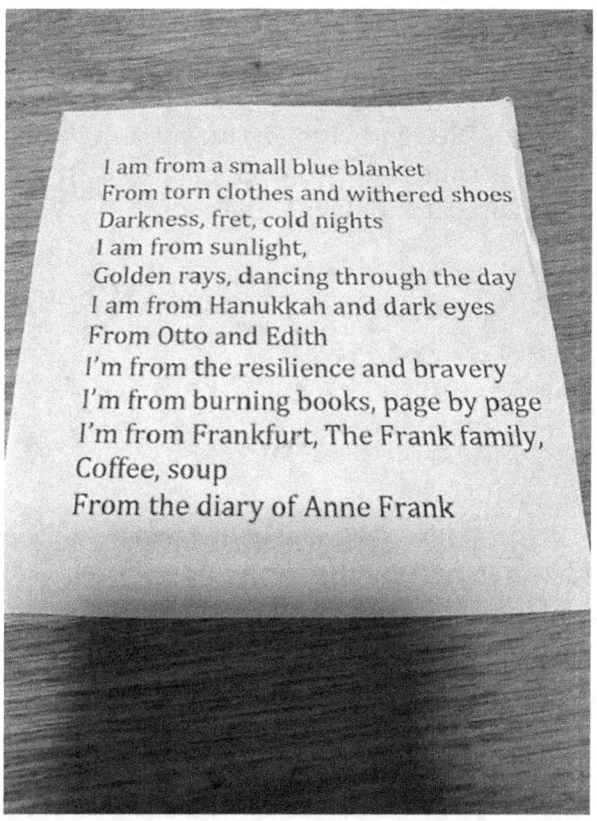

FIGURE 6.4 "I am from a small blue blanket" poem typed on paper.

I am From a Small Blue Blanket by Dana

I am from a small blue blanket
From torn clothes and withered shoes
Darkness, fret, cold nights
I am from sunlight,
Golden rays, dancing through the day
I am from Hanukkah and dark eyes
From Otto and Edith
I'm from the resilience and bravery
I'm from burning books, page by page
I'm from Frankfurt, the Frank family,
Coffee, soup
From the diary of Anne Frank

The examples of free verse poems below show how students use their own poetic techniques. In the first example, "Is this Freedom?" the poet asks hard questions about the true meaning of freedom. In the second, "Red and Blue," a student uses rhyme and a familiar children's church poem, beginning to craft her own perception of a Holocaust variation of the poem.

"Is this Freedom?" by Jasmin

Work makes you free
If that were true, why are there so many screams
The holes in the concrete walls
The blood that drips below
Reveals the horror hidden

Why must we take a shower for them
After they caused the conditions
Which made us so dirty

As we walk along in rows of one
No one dare break
Across the path as we walk
Barbed wire isn't able to hide
The horrid cries

"Red and Blue" by Katie

This is my home,
These are my people
I belong to this stone,
This is my steeple.

The cross is where
I have verses to share
But my clothes they tear.

Thrown in mud,
My faith stays true,
Only by blood,
The reds want my blue.

Because of my veins,
I am now in chains.
No explaining.
No reason.

It's a treason.

Paint chip poetry often blends rich emotion with color, as seen in the example below.

"Sullen Colors" by Veronica

A field of pretty orchids,
Now all smashed and bloodied.
They hide in a synagogue,
With their clothes all muddied.

The creaking of the floors shook them to life.
Looking at him, there was a trembling fear in his eyes.
Thousands of people are gone.
One last glance.

So many things to be said, such little time.
She messed up. But he was fading away.
His chest soaked in blood,
I can't forgive myself.

That crooked smile on the soldier's face.
This was meant to happen.
I was meant to lose him.
Their once bright world,
Now filled with sullen colors.

Teacher Tip

To make this poetry writing experience even more memorable and engaging, students can display their poems on decorative scrapbook paper backings and also make videos of themselves reading the poetry and placing these on QR Codes around the school or community so that others can listen to their poems. For this unit, students created kiosks with lovely scrapbook papers and framed poems, painted rocks with butterflies on one side, and a QR Code giving information about The Butterfly Project (https://thebutterflyprojectnow.org/), a call-to-action educational movement on the dangers of hatred and bigotry through Holocaust memorial art, on the other.

Expo visitors took a rock to place somewhere in the community to beautify the walkways and share information with those who picked up the rocks to discover the code on the back.

FIGURE 6.5 Bosnian Genocide Kiosk example.

Here is one student kiosk with information about the Bosnian Genocide on the whiteboard stand. Picture books written by students, the anchor text, and poetry surround the display (Figure 6.5).

Celebrating Deeper Learning Through Poetry

Step 4: Setting up the Expo

Students and teachers promoted the poetry expo event through *PeachJar* (n.d.), an app our school system uses to distribute news flyers for upcoming events through mass email to our families and community stakeholders. Students gathered their anchor texts, poetry and art journals, and butterfly rocks to place around their kiosks for expo attendees to see. They created title and overview descriptions on their kiosks using class notes throughout the unit of study to guide their presentations and to allow attendees to see at a glance which genocide they had researched. Students were presented as partners or trios based on their choice of genocide group.

Since students were required to be at the expo as part of their grade, we held the expo from noon until 1:00 on a school day so that community stakeholders could use their lunchtimes to attend and so that transportation did not become a barrier impacting any student's grade. At the student expo, tables were set up across the collaborative learning room. Each table held three kiosks, or presentation stations, that stakeholders could visit. Stakeholders were given one hour to move from station to station to ask students to share a 5-minute oral presentation of their learning and answer questions. This way, attendees could hear from each group of students as they moved throughout the expo room.

Students took great pride in sharing their poetry with others through oral readings and written displays. Through substantive conversations, they could freely articulate their discoveries, reactions, and the value of their learning beyond the walls of the classroom and school.

FIGURE 6.6 Students share their learning beside their display kiosks.

Attendees listen as students share their learning at the Poetry Expo in 2023 (Figure 6.6).

Beyond the Expo

Step 5: Reflections on Learning
After reflecting on our daytime Poetry Expo in 2023, teachers decided to offer an evening expo instead of a daytime expo, provided all students could secure transportation to the event. We wanted to take the poetry to the greater community so that citizens could come after work to the local coffee shop on

National Holocaust Remembrance Day (May 6, 2024) at 6:00 p.m. Teachers and students arrived, gathered outside with their framed poems in hand, and entered the coffee shop in one throng in flash mob style, taking the raised platform stage to read their poems one by one before placing them together on the table for attendees to read as each speaker concluded. A hush fell over the crowd as those present listened with attentive ears, snapping as applause after each speaker concluded. Tears filled the eyes of most listeners, standing with mouths agape, in awe of the power of the lines students shared.

FIGURE 6.7 Attendees of the Poetry Flash Mob listen to a student recite a poem.

Attendees listen as students share poems at the Poetry Flash Mob on Holocaust Remembrance Day at a local coffee shop. We discovered that the coffee shop attendees outnumbered the daytime expo attendees because all students had a family member who had transported them in attendance (Figure 6.7).

FIGURE 6.8 Table display of students' poems on genocide.

Student poets placed their poems on the table of our local coffee shop. Poems remained on display and became a symbol of the act of remembering on National Holocaust Remembrance Day (Figure 6.8).

How to Adapt This for Other Content Areas

Consider these steps to adapt the Poetry Expo to other content areas:

1) Decide on the most effective types of poetry for the student writing, then after the unit provide a 5-minute preview of each poem choice above by showing YouTube clips or sharing mentor poems in those formats. In this unit, the teacher offered free verse, Jenga block poetry, cento poetry, paint chip poetry, and Where I'm From poetry, but other content areas may wish to use other poetry forms, depending on the unit of study. For

example, math-related content poetry may use Fibonacci Sequence poems or poems that rely on a particular syllable count or numeric structure. Here is a bank of poetry types from which to choose from Writer's Digest (n.d.).

2) Build a base of Jenga blocks by creating words for the blocks using theme-related words and/or unit vocabulary for the blocks. You may cut these from magazines or print them on the computer, then glue them onto the blocks using one undercoat of glue and a few thin overcoats of glue or Matte Finish Mod Podge, a brand of decoupage glue.

3) Build a base of Cento sticks by searching for poems on the theme or content under study to find the Cento lines, then write the lines in permanent ink onto 8" craft sticks or tongue depressors, along with the poem's title and poet on the back of the stick.

4) Consider having students write mentor poems of several different types to keep in a class binder as mentor texts for the poetry preview and future study units. This way, students take lead roles in teaching others and create ownership of learning.

5) Create a rubric or other assessment tool that targets student success. Here is an example of a Poetry Writing Rubric that can be used across content areas (see Table 6.2).

TABLE 6.2 Poetry Writing Rubric

Criteria	Not attempted	Partially meets criteria but needs revision support	Reflects a strong grasp of concepts and attention to detail	Reflects a strong grasp of concepts and attention to detail
Poetic Elements	– Poem was not attempted	– Poetic elements are difficult to understand or not appropriate for the poem – Style of poetry is unclear or confusing – Figurative language is unclear or inappropriate for the poem – Mood is unclear or inappropriate for the poem	– Poetic elements are included but somewhat confusing to understand – Attempts the style of poetry, but somewhat confusing – Figurative language is somewhat unclear – Mood is unclear	– Poetic elements are included in the poem – Correctly uses the selected style of poetry – Figurative language is easy to understand – Mood is expressed	– Poetic elements are creative and enhance the story in the poem – Correctly uses the type of poetry creatively – Figurative language is easy to understand and enhances the poem – Mood is clearly expressed and enhances the poem
Content	– Poem was not attempted	– Theme is unclear or inappropriate for the poem – Topic is unclear, author does not care, or does not follow directions – Most details do not support the theme or topic	– The theme is somewhat difficult to understand – Topic is somewhat unclear, or the author does not care about the topic – Some details add to the story of the poem	– The theme of the poem is clear – The topic is clear, and the author cares about – All details add and support the story of the poem	– The theme of the poem is clear and creative – Topic is clear, demonstrates strong understanding, cares for the topic – Details significantly add to the story of the poem

(Continued)

TABLE 6.2 (Continued)

Criteria	Not attempted	Partially meets criteria but needs revision support	Reflects a strong grasp of concepts and attention to detail	Reflects a strong grasp of concepts and attention to detail
Language Word Choice	– Poem was not attempted	– Word choice lacks verbiage of genocide	– At least one word suggests verbiage of genocide	– At least two words suggest verbiage of genocide	– More than two words suggest verbiage of genocide
Presentation & Publication	– Poem was not attempted	– Handwritten poem is difficult to read Or – Typed font, style, and color are inappropriate or difficult to read	– Handwritten poem is mostly legible Or – Typed poem has two or more poor choices in font, style, or color	– Handwritten poem is legible. Or – Typed poem has one font, style, or color choice that is difficult to read	– Handwritten poem is legible and pleasing to read Or – The typed poem has a good font, style, and color choice.

Notes

1. Accessible at: www.hmd.org.uk/resource/the-butterfly-by-pavel-friedmann
2. Johnson, K. (2023). *Cento video* [Video]. YouTube. https://youtu.be/vEkvX87z_20
3. Johnson, K. (2023). *Paint chip video* [Video]. YouTube. https://youtu.be/vxHRIIbe1vk
4. Johnson, K. (2024). *Jenga block video* [Video]. YouTube. https://youtu.be/6CWlHuQgqjl
5. The Quiet Creative (2020). *Free verse poems* [Video]. YouTube. https://youtu.be/GnIwOn94uJs?si=MaMTv2TKMi6drex8
6. Personal and Teacher Channel. (2020). *Where I'm from poems* [Video]. YouTube. https://youtu.be/iT0GSZXyOII?si=wCXZ9DcdkVEpx98W

Bibliography

Amazon. (n.d.). *Paint chip poetry: A game of color and wordplay.* www.amazon.com/Paint-Chip-Poetry-Color-Wordplay

Amazon. (n.d.). *Hasbro gaming hardwood Jenga: Classic stacking game, holiday toy stocking stuffers.* www.amazon.com/Hasbro-Gaming-Hardwood-Stacking-Stuffers/

Forchuk, L. (1991). *Nobody's child*. Collins.

Gustafson, A. (2021, November 10). *Unmasking the mythical narrative surrounding the five-paragraph essay*. National Council of Teachers of English. https://ncte.org/blog/2021/11/unmasking-mythical-narrative-surrounding-five-paragraph-essay/

Harden, B. (2012). *Escape from Camp 14: One man's remarkable odyssey from North Korea to freedom in the West*. Viking.

Holocaust Memorial Day Trust. (n.d.). *The butterfly by Pavel Friedmann* [Resource]. Holocaust Memorial Day Trust. www.hmd.org.uk/resource/the-butterfly-by-pavel-friedmann

Jansen, H. (2006). *Over a thousand hills I walk with you* (E. et al..). Carolrhoda Books. (Original work published 2002).

McCormick, P. (2012). *Never fall down*. Balzer Bray.

PeachJar. (n.d.). *PeachJar* (Version x.x) [Mobile app]. App Store. www.peachjar.com

Sabic-El-Rayess, A., & Sullivan, L. (2020). T*he cat I never named: A true story of love, war, and survival.* Bloomsbury YA.

Stanton, G. H. (1996). The ten stages of genocide. Genocide Watch. https://genocidewatch.net/genocide-2/8-stages-of-genocide/

United Nations. (n.d.). *The 17 goals*. https://sdgs.un.org/goals

Vazquez, A. (2023). Coming home: A reflection on the gift of poetry. *English Journal*, 112(4), 51–57.

Wiesel, E. (2006). *Night* (M. Wiesel, Trans.). Hill and Wang. (Original work published 1958).

Writer's Digest. (n.d.). *Poetic forms*. www.writersdigest.com/write-better-poetry/poetic-forms

7

Reflecting Back and Moving Forward

Anna J. Small Roseboro and Sarah J. Donovan

Collaborating on this publication, we five English language arts teachers learned more about what makes instruction humanizing. We worked with our colleagues in other content areas to explore writing poetry as an assessment. We learned so much about what writing poetry about natural hazards, first aid, and civil rights, for example, can do for our understanding of people in general, and teenagers in particular. In Georgia, Iowa, Maryland, Michigan, and Oklahoma, we met students with rich variations in learning styles, home or heart languages, race, religion, and regionality. The students' and their poetry became our teachers as we invited their whole being and linguistic repertoires into the classroom.

We compiled the eclectic chapters to enable you, our readers and colleagues, to teach in a humanizing way and to interact with students as unique and welcome members of our learning community. We designed the lessons in this collection to explore student learning in ways that consider who they are, what we teach, and how we can better reach them as they reach out to one another in lessons with guided choices. As experienced educators, we know that class time is valuable; we have striven to design lessons that maximize class time and reduce teacher homework time while concurrently increasing student learning and teacher learning about teaching.

Common Features in our Chapters

You will have noticed that each chapter has standard features, but each is unique because we, the contributing authors, have had different experiences in different parts of the country. The lessons each focus on other content areas but describe in detail ways to invite your students to write poems to show what they know about what you are teaching and what they are expected to know by the end of the course or school year. The poems they write are as revealing as a quiz, test, or exam can be to show students' levels of learning and understanding, as well as their interests and skills. You can measure or assess student learning by paying attention to the content specifics the students include in their poems.

As you reflect on what you have discovered, you will notice allusions to available resources, class time management, homework design, and extended learning opportunities that enrich and encourage collaboration inside and outside the classroom. When you implement the strategies, you will find that your students bring valuable experiences to the school that aid their learning, that of you, the teacher, and their classmates. That's what makes this approach humanizing. Each person has something to offer, and the lessons here invite and respect those offerings in multiple ways, using pen, paper, oral, and multimedia presentations. Our units suggest ways to share what students learn in other settings, such as e-books, videos, and community outreach projects.

Key concepts flow through the book to assure you that implementing these strategies expands and enriches your instruction practices in ways you can articulate with those who challenge your adding poetry assignments in non-English language arts courses.

- Anna, the value of visualizing and personalizing learning
- Sarah, the humanizing and comprehension value of these assignments
- Barbara, honing research and inquiry skills and using gathered information in poetry
- Gayle, developing academic language through poetic contexts and connections
- Kim, ways to share student learning and invite community to write poems

Whether you teach upper elementary, middle, or high school, content in your curriculum can be enriched as students synthesize what they know, think, and envision in poems you assign them to write. Consider the S.T.R.E.A.M. of courses taught in schools across the nation:

- Sciences, Social Studies, Software Development, Speech Communications
- Technology, Theater Arts, Trades
- Reflecting on Religion, Faiths, Cultures, and Retail Management
- Ecology, Economics, Energy, Engineering, and English Language Arts
- Accounting, Anthropology, Architecture, Athletics, Arts and Design
- Mass Communication, Mathematics, Medicine, Money Management, and Music

Table 7.1 compiles the various courses offered in the districts where our team members teach or have taught. Following the table, you will see our chapters' general time charts and suggested poem forms and styles you may choose to use to inspire research and sharing, measure interest, and learn and understand the courses you teach.

TABLE 7.1 Range of Courses Taught in the Authors' Local High Schools

Business	Family & Consumer Science	Health Occupations First Aid	Industrial Technology Building Trades
Accounting Business Leadership Business Law Marketing Personal Finance Marketing	Child Development Consumer Science Culinary Arts Independent Living	Ethics Health Occupations Human Relations Nurse Aide (CNA)	Carpentry Capstone/Engineering Fabrication Industrial Skills Welding/Metal

English Language Arts	Fine Arts	Languages	Maths
American Literature Advanced Placement Composition Advanced Placement Literature Creative Writing Drama Independent Reading Journalism Public Speaking Publications World Literature	Band Ceramics Choir Concert/Show Dance Digital Design Digital Photography Foundations of Art Graphic Art Painting Orchestra Studio Art Video Media Arts	Arabic Chinese Dutch French German Italian Latin Spanish American Sign Language	Algebra Calculus College Math Geometry Pre-Calculus Integrated Math Transitions to Algebra

Physical Education	Science	Agriculture	Fashion & Design
Health Fitness Health Nutrition Human Physiology Personal Strength Physical Education Team PE	Astronomy Biology Geology Chemistry Physics Physical Science	Agribusiness Agricultural Engineering Agronomy Animal Systems Farm Management Plant and Soil Sciences Power and Technology	Business Construction Design Illustration Management Ornamentation Pattern Making Textile

Over the years, educators nationwide have assembled poetry prompts that work well in content areas because of their forms. For example, in math, the Fibonacci sequence or Fib poems (Poetry Society of Indiana, n.d.).named for this famous mathematician are structured so that the number of syllables in each line equals the total number of syllables in the preceding two lines. Students must do the math to create the poem. Assigning the creation of poems such as haiku, tanka, and Nonet, poems structured by numbers, provides opportunities for teachers to discover what students know about specific topics as learners practice skills needed for solving problems in math classes.

Consider shaping poems based on the outlines of famous historical sites or in the shape of animals or trees, using vocabulary words and facts from the content areas. Classroom teachers who wish to provide a platform for student discovery and presentation may choose the golden shovel or strike-out poems because these styles require students to pull lines from other readings. Here is a place to look for poetry forms that may be a good fit for various subject areas: www.writersdigest.com/write-better-poetry/poetic-forms. The fun will confirm the value of such creative reviews and presentations. Soon, students will realize and appreciate how often their poems help other learners: you, their teachers, and their classmates.

Inviting students to show what they know and are learning can be a breeze as they incorporate carefully selected words, phrases, and sentences into short pieces lined up on the page in purposeful patterns. And, you saw in most chapters that this guided choice work need not be graded to be effective. Most lessons are designed to start and finish in steps that can be completed in a 45-55 minute time chunk.

Note that many of us described timing lessons with:

- ♦ 15-18 minutes for gathering information through recall or research
- ♦ 10-12 minutes for introducing poetry prompt and viewing sample or model texts

- 15-18 minutes for students to draft their poems to show their thinking about the topic
- 3-5 minutes to share poems and write exit slip stating what they learned during class time

The most critical assessment for educators is to see our students beam as we write with them, watch them attend to the tasks, read what they write, listen to their work with one another, and proudly present their poems. Most students are successful with these assignments and, therefore, trust us more when we give them other challenging tasks that expand and deepen their learning as the school year unfolds.

Other Times to Write Poetry

Perhaps nothing was more challenging than when "unfold" meant schools closed during the pandemic. Sarah's students wrote a poem online for a day in April 2020. Daily online writing was a way to stay connected to school and one another. Sarah's professional learning community (PLC) of English language arts, Maths, Social Studies, Physical Education, Computers, Music, and World Languages collaborated to develop prompts to explore different content areas. One seventh-grader posted this Nonet, a nine-line poem about healthcare workers:

> Working hard day and night just to help,
> caring, and supporting everyone,
> no expectations, no limits.
> They are strong, brave, and good.
> Saving us, their work.
> Big thanks to the
> Health workers,
> doctors,
> you.

Sometimes, current events require teachers to pause their unit plans and offer time for students to process what happened.

What happened may be something local to your community, like the death of a student or faculty member. What happened may be the loss of a beloved athlete, like when Kobe Bryant died tragically. Grief will impact communities and students in different ways. You may invite students to write about grief from a distance using an epistle prompt. An epistle is a letter. Sarah invited students to write a letter to something or someone they have lost. Some students wrote about concrete objects, like the loss of a toy, while others wrote about abstract loss, like their childhood, overwhelmed by the demands of junior high. This student had recently moved to Sarah's school and was missing home.

> Dear Hayward,
>
> I never knew how precious you were to me
> Until I moved away
> Until I watched you fading behind me,
> in the car, headed for an unknown location
> Until I realized the strength you built in me
> OH! I never knew how precious you were to me,
>   but now
> I miss the school I went to, teeming with familiar faces
> Those friends and enemies who all lived side by side
> Who made the school a better place
> I miss my friends you gave me
> Those friends who stuck by me, trudged along with me
> Those friends I will never let go
> I miss the teachers of that sacred school
> The band teacher who smiled while yelling at us for
>   playing the wrong notes, baton flying
> The kind P.E. teacher who was a veteran and looked
>   dead serious on the outside
> I miss your bustling community, however small it was
> Those people who all knew each other
> Those people who smiled often Oh!
> I never knew how precious you were to you, but now
> I miss the feet of snow piled upon your streets
> That snow perfect for sledding
> That snow perfect for playing outside while time flies by

> I miss your cold weather
> Which rendered ice sculptures possible
> Which rendered slippery sledding paths possible Oh!
> I never knew how precious you were to me, but now
> I treasure you I take pride in being able to relate you
> I will always remember you, with all my heart
> And we will, although we may be far apart, always be
>   connected with our souls

Imagine taking a break from your content or swapping your bellringer for a reflective prompt. Imagine what you can learn about your students and them from one another in ten minutes of writing, from an invitation to imagine a poem. For more prompts to build community, see *90 Ways of Community: Nurturing Safe & Inclusive Classrooms Writing One Poem at a Time* (Donovan et al., 2024).

An Uncovering Approach to Content

As you share what you are exploring here in *Assessing Students with Poetry Writing Across Content Areas: Humanizing Formative Assessment for Grades 6-12,* you, too, will find yourself expanding and deepening your understanding of students as you collaborate with others in your education circle to implement the strategies we offer in this rich trove of lessons designed for diverse student bodies.

Rosen (1981) refers to writing poetry as opening up a space in which youth can reflect upon the world, their values, and the place of those values in the world. As you begin incorporating writing poetry into your assignments, you will likely notice students feeling more comfortable using one another's names, recognizing their expertise, finding connections among themselves and across the content areas, and, most importantly, building trust in one another. You will be pleased with the shift in your pedagogy from "delivering" or "covering" content to cocreating and uncovering knowledge as you and your students learn together.

As you begin to adapt these lessons with other poem forms and topics, we want to point out something important about structuring some of these lessons. The mentor texts we include are not "algorithms for writing a new text in the way that a worked-out algebra problem may be a model for solving new problems of the same type" (Charney & Carlson, 1995, p. 91). While serving a useful purpose in aiding writers in beginning a poem or synthesizing new knowledge with prior knowledge, showing models is just one strategy. They need not be the only template students use when writing. When possible, offer a few mentor texts and invite students to throw out the model completely to invent a new poem, try their own form, and craft another algorithm for writing.

Equally gratifying is that you will find that high-order skills, such as learning about choice and embracing unpredictability, will increase the confidence in you and your students when they see you are poised to try new writing tasks. That's why we encourage you to model this vulnerability in your classroom. And the more guided choices you offer, the more likely you and your students will develop an eagerness to incorporate their lived experiences, their choice of vocabulary and grammar patterns, and their fund of knowledge into other assignments that leave the door open for such information. In this book, you have seen multiple ways knowledge can be transferred as well as recalled and transmitted.

Continuing Your Poetic Journey

We, the co-authors of this book, have been writing poetry with students for many years, and we have developed additional resources to help teachers imagine how writing poetry can support learning. Please look at our open-access resources *90 Ways of Community: Nurturing Safe & Inclusive Classrooms Writing One Poem at a Time* and *Words That Mend: The Transformative Power of Writing Poetry for Teachers, Students, and Community Wellbeing*. These books include an expansive selection of poetry forms and mentor texts that will likely spark ideas for your classroom.

From experience, we know that teachers writing poetry with students develop new ideas on inquiry with poetry, so we encourage you to share with other educators what you are creating in your practice. Reach out to your local teaching affiliate of your content area (e.g., National Council for Social Studies, National Council of Teachers of Mathematics, and National Science Teaching Association) to propose a conference session or article for their journal. Reach out to us with stories of how the poetry writing is going. We'd love to hear from you and feature your story in our poetry networks.

> When we construct schemes for teaching students to think and to use language, we should not overlook the power of the poetic for helping them think through the full range of the human agenda, not only in the broad, relatively comfortable contours of academic discourse but in the tighter, more difficult regions of mental and physical experience as well. When the medium is language, it is through poetic thinking and poetry that young people, and finally all of us, come to face what we cannot face, to know what we cannot know, and to say what we have no idea how to say.
>
> (Tremmel, 1992, p. 30)

The selections made and poems created reveal the students' interest and understanding to teachers. Seeing and hearing the poems also exposes what needs to be retaught before a high-impact test or exam. Teachers have some say in what is done in the classroom, even when they cannot control what is on tests and exams. Since it is clear that students who write regularly retain information longer and because poems both display learning and expose misunderstandings, assigning ungraded poetry is just another tool to use for teaching.

Our Acrostic Poem – HUMANIZING ASSESSMENT

H	Handle with care	A	Attend to process over product
U	Understand each one	S	Share your meaning-making
M	Minimize grading	S	Stimulate sensitivity
A	Anticipate challenge	E	Energize engagement
N	Nurture collaboration	S	Sketch new pathways
I	Inspire individualism	S	Seek creativity
Z	Zealously celebrate	M	Maximize authenticity
I	Invite opinion	E	Electrify learning
N	Neutralize worry	N	Now you know
G	Go for it!	T	Try it. You'll like it!

References

Charney, D. H., & Carlson, R. A. (1995). Learning to write in a genre: What student writers take from model texts. *Research in the Teaching of English, 29*(1), 88–125.

Donovan, S. J., Daley, M., & Ingram, M. Y. (2024). *90 ways of community: Nurturing safe & inclusive classrooms writing one poem at a time.* Seela Books.

Poetry Society of Indiana. (n.d.). Fibonacci poem. Poetry Society of Indiana. www.poetrysocietyofindiana.org/blog/fibonacci-poem

Rosen, M. (1981). Chivvy. In R. McGough & M. Rosen (Eds.), *You tell me* (p. 88). Puffin.

Tremmel, R. (1992). Making the return move: Secondary students thinking poetically and writing poetry. *The Journal of Aesthetic Education, 26*(2), 17–30. www.jstor.org/stable/3332920

For Product Safety Concerns and Information please contact our EU representative GPSR@taylorandfrancis.com
Taylor & Francis Verlag GmbH, Kaufingerstraße 24, 80331 München, Germany

www.ingramcontent.com/pod-product-compliance
Lightning Source LLC
Chambersburg PA
CBHW062143300426
44115CB00012BA/2018